Zacharias Tanee Fomum

Enjoying The Premarital Life

Éditions du Livre Chrétien
4, rue du Révérend Père Cloarec
92400 Courbevoie France
editionlivrechretien@gmail.com

In this book I have said it all as it is.

I have held nothing back

© Zacharias Tanee Fomum, 1984

All Rights Reserved

Pbublished by :

EDITIONS DU LIVRE CHRÉTIEN

4, rue du Révérend Père Cloarec

92400 Courbevoie - FRANCE

Tél : (33) 9 52 29 27 72

Email : editionlivrechretien@gmail.com

I dedicate this book to

All the people of all ages

Who yearn for enjoyment

In the sexual life

Unless otherwise stated, the Scripture quotations in this book are taken from the **Revised Standard Version** *of the Holy Bible, the British Edition.*

Table Of Contents

Preface 9

Enjoying The Sexual Life? 10

God The Creator Of Sex 15

The Bible: The Manufacturer's Handbook On Sex 18

The Abuse Of The Sexual Life 21
    Petting and pornography 21
    Masturbation 24
    Fornication 25
    Adultery 36
    Homosexuality 38

Human Attempts At Solving The Problem 45
    Human attempts 46
    What of the past? 47
    What of the future? 48

God's Solution To The Problem 52
    The incarnation 53
    The death of christ 54
    The resurrection of christ 57
    The enthronement of christ 58

Examples Of God's Solution To The Problem 64
    Forgiven and healed! 64
    I am so changed 74
    Saved, healed and truly liberated 78
    I found peace, hope and happiness 84

Truly freed 90
You Can Become A Virgin Again 102
    Getting into christ... 103
Enjoying The Sexual Life.. 105
    Come Now To Jesus.. 107
Very important 109
About the author... 113

Preface

This book, **"Enjoying the Premarital Life,"** is the first of three books in the series entitled: *"God, Sex, and You."*

The second book in this series is entitled: "Enjoying the Choice of Your Marriage Partner," while the third book in this series is entitled: "Enjoying the Married Life."

Book one continues in book two and book three brings the theme to a climax. To have a balanced and complete view of what God has given us on the subject, we encourage you to read books two and three as well.

We send this book out with faith that you will soon discover that it is the book for you, your parents, your children, your friends and all whom you know, and that you will do all you can to put it within their reach.

If you have been blessed, encouraged, challenged, provoked or made angry by the contents of this book, please write to me about how you feel.

God bless you!

1st February, 1984

Dr. Zacharias TANEE FOMUM

P.O. Box 6090

Yaounde, CAMEROON

Chapter 1

Enjoying The Sexual Life?

I had just finished the message when a young man walked up to me. He was tall, slim and very handsome. He took me aside and quietly told me his story. This is what he said: "I came to this city six years ago and soon found a good job since I was very well-qualified. I set out to enjoy myself with girls. At first, it was all so good. I was like a king — liked, loved and adored. I went from one girl to another and then decided to conquer as many of them as I could. I thought to myself that the more girls I knew the happier I would become. Things continued like that for some time. Sometimes I contacted venereal diseases from the girls, but I was able to get treated very soon.

One unfortunate day, I met with one girl and this contact gave me a more serious disease. I have had this disease for over four years now. I have visited many hospitals and private clinics, but I have not been treated. The symptoms of the disease are increasing. At the moment I am beginning to lose my manly powers. I feel horrible. How shall I face the future if my manhood is not restored? To make things more difficult for me, my parents have got a young wife for me in the village. She is young, fresh and innocent. They will soon send her to me. What shall I do? Sometimes I think that the best thing to do is to go and throw myself into the sea and end it all. I am not enjoying life. Is there any hope for me?"

****

"Please Sir, can I talk to you?" I turned and faced the young woman who stood before me. She was about 26 years old, well-dressed and sophisticated. When I was able to listen to her, this is what she said to me: "When I was a student in the High School, I went out to seek experience because many of my friends were doing that. In the course of it I got pregnant. The boy who made me pregnant gave me money and I got an experienced hospital attendant to help me to commit an abortion. Many people did not know about my pregnancy and, so, I was able to continue life as normal after the abortion was committed.

Then four years ago I got married. We have been waiting and waiting in vain for our baby to be conceived. Each month I say to myself, "It will happen this month," but nothing happens. Each time I have my monthly period, I hate myself and a voice inside me says, "You murdered your first child, why should God give you another one?"

I do not know what to do with myself. I hate all the boys who had sexual relationships with me. I hate the boy who made me pregnant. Above all, I hate myself. I am useless. What can I do with myself? I have never told my husband that I once committed an abortion. I instead lied to him that he was the first man in my life. I fear that someday he will know the truth and our marriage will end.

You have talked about the love of God for abortionists. Can that love include me?"

****

He was 19 and in the High School. He accepted no criticism. He did everything to prove that he was right. He did everything to draw attention to himself. Then one day, he confided in me. This is what he said: "I am very lonely. I do not know who my father is. It is as if I came from nowhere. Each time I ask my mother to show me my father, or at least to tell me his name, she just looks into the air and says nothing. I feel like taking up a gun and shooting her and then shooting myself, and then it will be a happy end."

*****

She was the most intelligent student in the entire tribe. Normally, girls were not allowed to go to the University in this tribe. The people could not afford it and, besides, they thought that things might go wrong with the girls in the course of the many years at school. Because she was so brilliant, her teachers pleaded with her parents to relent and let her be educated. They gave in and sacrificially sent her to Remareke University in Nadagu. It was the early days and the laws of that University were strict. No unmarried girl who was pregnant could continue in that University. She went in the way of the wayward and an "accident" occurred. She was dismissed and sent back home without the diploma she had gone to seek. The parents were heartbroken. The teachers were disillusioned and the villagers named her baby "Diploma."

****

I was visiting one country on a scientific tour. At the earliest opportunity, I made contact with the believers and was invited to speak at a meeting arranged particularly for wives of the University teachers. At the close of the meeting, an elegant lady of about forty-five asked if she could have a private talk with me. We arranged a meeting for the next day. At that meeting, I just sat for two hours while she poured out her sad story. This is what she told me: "I was a virgin at the time of my marriage and all through my life, my husband has been the only man in my life. I loved him and trusted him. However, five years ago, I discovered that he had been untrue to me for all the years of our married life and had children with other women. I saw the children and they all resembled him. From then on, my heart was broken and my deep love for him turned into bitter hatred. He apologized to me and was truly repentant, but my heart was closed to him. Everyday I sit at table opposite him and the sight of him makes me feel like ending my life and his own. We have money, position, respect from people, everything we need but, finally, we have nothing."

****

"I wish I had not married you," said he in anger to her. "You are cold and not responsive. My girlfriends were wonderful. How can I forget Caroline or Josephine or sweet Vivian? They knew how to go about these things and here am I doomed to live with a frozen being. What shall I do? You will stay at home and be cold to yourself. I will go out and have fun and, some day, it will be goodbye."

****

She walked into his apartment. However, today she was not as gay and as confident as she normally used to be. A distance seemed to have built in between them. She was afraid to get near him. There was a slight dislike in his attitude towards her. "John, I have something to say to you, but I am afraid. I hope when you will have heard it, you will not be angry and unhappy. May I say it?" "Say it at once," was his answer. "Please John, I cannot see my period. It is now seven days overdue and I am hopelessly worried and frightened. What shall we do? Maybe the thing we feared has happened."

"Do not tell me your stupid nonsense," replied John. "Go and look for your period and be sure to find it. Why do you come to me? How can I be sure that I am responsible? Is there any guarantee that you did not give yourself to other boys as you gave yourself so easily to me? So I am the fool you think should take the responsibility? You are mistaken. Leave my house at once and never come back. I do not want to see you any more."

The above are real life stories. As I heard them from one of the parties involved in each case I could not help asking the question, "Were they really enjoying the sexual life?" They had all gone into it with the hope that they would enjoy it, but did they accomplish their purpose?

The rest of the book is about the problems involved in trying to enjoy the sexual life, and the answer to lasting happiness in the sexual life. Come with me and let us together face the issues involved, and then face the timeless answer to these problems.

Chapter 2

God The Creator Of Sex

God created man with the sexual capacity. He could have created him without sex organs and without the capacity to respond in the sexual realm. However, in His eternal wisdom, He decided that the sexual life was good for the people He had created and so He put this capacity into them. There is nothing wrong with the sexual life. He approved of it. In the Bible He says:

"Enjoy life with the wife whom you love,

all the days of your vain life

which he has given you under the sun,

because that is your portion in life

and in your toil at which you toil under the sun"

(Ecclesiastes 9:9).

He further says,

"Drink water from your own cistern

flowing water from your own well.

Should your springs be scattered abroad,

streams of water in the streets?

Let them be for yourself alone,

and not for strangers with you.

Let your fountain be blessed,

and rejoice in the wife of your youth,

a lovely hind, a graceful doe.

Let her affection fill you at all times with delight,

be infatuated always with her love.

Why should you be infatuated, my son, with a loose woman and embrace the bosom of an adventuress?

For a man's ways are before the eyes of the Lord,

and he watches all his paths.

The iniquities of the wicked ensnare him,

and he is caught in the toils of his sin.

He dies for lack of discipline,

and because of his great folly he is lost"

(Proverbs 5: 15-23).

He again says,

"*Therefore a man leaves his father and his mother and cleaves to his wife, and they become one flesh*" (Genesis 2.24).

The God who created sex is saying, "Get properly married to a wife of your own. After you are married, have the maximum amount of sex possible. After you are married, enjoy sex with your partner to the highest degree that is possible. After you are married, fill your partner with the highest sexual pleasure possible and let your partner fill you with the highest degree possible."

God intends that people SHOULD derive the highest sexual pleasure that can be obtained, provided that this is done under the simple condition that he has laid down.

We must immediately ask, "What is that simple condition that God has laid down under which people may enter into all the sexual pleasure that is possible?"

Chapter 3

The Bible: The Manufacturer's Handbook On Sex

When the Mercedes Benz Company manufactures a brand new car, they produce a manufacturer's guide along with it. This book contains information about the car and this information includes the condition under which the car is to be used for maximum durability, safety and comfort. If a person were to buy a brand new car and then say to himself, "I have the car, I do not care about what the manufacturer says, I will not read his guide, I will not obey his instruction, I must go away at once and use the car, after all, I can manage." Such a person might forget to put engine oil into the car and soon the engine would knock and the car would be ruined. He might accelerate instead of braking and be involved in a car accident that would cost him his car and his life. He might, on the other hand, go for the rest of his life with scars or broken parts of the body that speak of his refusal to take the manufacturer's instructions seriously.

Sexual life is like a Mercedes Benz car. God is the Manufacturer. The Manufacturer's Guide on the sexual life is the Bible. One of the fundamental instructions in the Manufacturer's Guide on the sexual life says that a man may engage in sexual relationship with a woman only after the two are properly married, and that all sexual relationships before or outside of marriage are strictly forbidden.

This instruction is given for the good of those who would be involved in the sexual life.

There are a number of questions that a person needs to face very honestly before he or she is involved in any sexual relationship:

1. Does God approve of this relationship? If the answer is, "No," then the relationship should not be entered into. There are two reasons why it must not be attempted at all. First of all, if God does not approve of it, He will bring all who transgress His commandment to judgment on the last day. Secondly, because He forbids only what is harmful to man, all who engage in what He has forbidden will find that, in the long run, they are the losers.

2. Will this relationship bring happiness to me now, during all of my earthly life and in my life after this world? If the relationship brings happiness for a few minutes, hours, days or months, but is not sure to bring happiness in all of the future on earth or in the world to come, it should not be engaged in.

3. Will this relationship bring happiness to the one who is involved with me in it during all of the person's earthly life and in the life to come? If the relationship will bring happiness to the person for a few minutes, hours, days or months but will not bring happiness to the person in all of the future on earth and in the world to come, it should not be entered into.

4. Would this relationship bring happiness to my parents and the parents of the one involved in it with me, were they to know about it? If it would not bring happiness to the parents and relatives of those who are involved in the relationship, it should not be entered into.
5. Will this relationship be a blessing to any children that may come into the world as a result of it? If the relationship is likely to make any children who are born as a result of it unhappy, it should not be entered into.
6. Will this relationship bring a blessing on my community, nation, continent and world? If it will not bring a blessing on the community, nation, continent and world, it should not be entered into.

Chapter 4

The Abuse Of The Sexual Life

Although the Manufacturer's Guide on the sexual life - the Bible - states the Manufacturer's mind about the sexual life: how it may be entered into and how it may be maintained so that it is a blessing, many people have purposefully or ignorantly gone contrary to the Manufacturer's Guide on the sexual life. This abuse of the sexual life can be put into five main classes.

PETTING AND PORNOGRAPHY

There are some people who kiss people of the opposite sex who are not their wives. They embrace them and touch their bodies all over, touching what should not be touched and exciting what they should not excite. They may not enter into the full sexual act. This is an abuse of the sexual life. The reasons for this are immediately obvious. We shall briefly look at them but, before that, let us say that others fill their minds with sexual stories from dirty books and magazines or films. The overall effect is like that of petting.

First of all, God does not approve of this kind of sexual relationship. It leads to sexual sins in thought. The Lord Jesus said, "*You have heard that it was said, 'You shall not commit adultery.' But I say to you that every one who looks at a woman lustfully has already committed adultery with her in his heart*" (Matthew 5. 27-28). Because petting and the reading of dirty books or the looking at sexy pictures and the like lead to adultery and fornication in thought, they are an abuse of the sexual life. God will punish all who are involved in such relationships in the lake of fire. The Bible says, "*Blessed are the pure in heart, for they shall see God*" (Matthew 5 : 8). When a person's thoughts are filled with lust because of petting and the like, he is wooing God's judgment and He will not let such people go unpunished.

Secondly, the relationship of petting – touching parts of the body that you should not touch and kissing people that you should not kiss, cannot be to your advantage or to the person's advantage. You may think that you want to kiss and stop at kissing, to embrace and stop at embracing, to touch and stop at touching. However, you are joking with fire. The sexual desire is very strong. You are likely to go beyond the point at which you intended to stop. You may think that you will stop just at touching, but you might soon find that touching made you desire more and you landed into masturbation, fornication or adultery, with all their dreadful consequences. The only safety lies in not kissing, not touching and not reading any dirty books. "Prevention is better than cure."

Thirdly, it may ruin your future marriage. There are a number of ways by which petting can do this:- First of all, many boys will lose respect for any girl who allows them to kiss her and touch the intimate parts of her body before marriage. Men long for unconquered territory. If he has already touched you all over, he is most likely to prefer a girl whom he has not touched. To him you are already conquered. You are second-class property. He has little to look forward to. He wants someone else. Secondly, a man tends not to trust a girl to whose body he has had access. Many men say to themselves, "She let me touch her this far. Maybe she has allowed other men to touch her that far and perhaps further. How can I be sure that I am the only one whom she allows to do this to her?" Such a girl would drop on the marriage scale. Even if he later on marries her, he will always have it in his mind that she is not totally out of the reach of other men. Thirdly, petting may ruin a future marriage in two other ways: A boy or girl who was kissed, caressed and touched by X, Y, Z must have been kissed, caressed and touched in different ways; each person kissing, caressing, touching and exciting her body differently. In marriage, the husband may not be able to excite her body to the same degree that all the people who petted her did, and this would limit the degree of sexual enjoyment possible for her. It is obvious that it will not be possible to find a partner who would caress you the way X, Y and Z did. Even in marriage you may be yearning for the touches of one or two of these people, and how can you be happy with the touches of your wife or husband which may be different from these? If, on the other hand, you were untouched, you would gladly accept what you have from your partner and be satisfied with it. A person who was kissed and caressed by different people is more prone to temptations in the realm of adultery than the one who only knew these things in marriage and with his or her partner.

Fourthly, there are diseases that are communicated through kissing. Syphilis can be communicated through kissing. Tuberculosis can also be communicated through kissing. Leprosy can be communicated through touching. The sin of petting carries with it the above health hazards, plus others like

- tonsillitis
- common cold
- common sore
- viral hepatitis
- gingivitis
- meningocaocal meningitis
- etc.

These diseases that can be spread through kissing are a burden to the community, nation, continent and world.

MASTURBATION

Masturbation is personal excitation towards some kind of sexual climax without a sex partner. This is a sexual perversion, for God meant the sexual relationship to be carried out between a married man and his wife. Masturbation is against the Manufacturer's Guide on the sexual life, and God forbids it. The Manufacturer's Guide says, *"Do you not know that the unrighteous will not inherit the kingdom of God? Do not be deceived; neither the immoral, nor idolaters, nor adulterers, nor sexual perverts, nor thieves, nor the greedy, nor drunkards, nor revilers, nor robbers will inherit the kingdom of God"* (I Corinthians 6: 9-10). All those who break God's law by masturbating will have their part in the lake of fire. That will be their full pay.

Masturbation also leads to guilt and impure thoughts, and could lead to many psychological disorders. Many who start on the way of masturbation find that the habit soon binds them and they struggle in vain to set themselves free. Some find it a "safe" way of sexual enjoyment before marriage, but they wake up to find out that the habit has got hold of them so much so that even in marriage they would prefer sexual pleasure through masturbation rather than with their partners.

No one who is truly wise can afford to abuse himself in this way. Those who masturbate are not enjoying the sexual life. Rather, they are laying a sad foundation for the future. Such a foundation will greatly hinder their possibility of having a truly satisfying sexual life in marriage.

FORNICATION

Fornication is a sexual relationship between two people neither of whom is married. If an unmarried boy goes to bed with an unmarried girl, they commit the sin of fornication.

Fornication is against the Manufacturer's Guide for the sexual life. God will punish all fornicators. The Manufacturer's Guide, the Bible, says, *"Now, the works of the flesh are plain: fornication, impurity, licentiousness, idolatry, sorcery, enmity, strife, jealousy, anger, selfishness, dissension, party spirit, envy, drunkenness, carousing, and the like. I warn you, as I warned you before, that those who do such things shall not inherit the kingdom of God"* (Galatians 5: 19-21). The Bible further says, *"But as for the cowardly, the faithless, the polluted, as for murderers, fornicators, sorcerers, idolaters, and all liars, their lot shall be in the lake that burns with fire and sulphur, which is the second death"* (Revelation 21:8).

Fornication is not only a sin against God. Its consequences are far-reaching. We shall look at some of these consequences:

1. Venereal Diseases and Their Tragic Consequences

Diseases like the ones that were underlined under kissing can be contacted during fornication. In addition, there are venereal diseases that can be contacted in the act of fornication. Think of a healthy young man who commits the sin of fornication with a girl who has a venereal disease such as syphilis. This disease is transmitted to the young man. The disease may not be properly treated in the young man, such that it develops and produces secondary and perhaps tertiary characteristics. Some of these characteristics may be experienced in the first year, while others may only appear ten years later. However, whether the penalty for the act is visible soon or visible after ten years, it comes from uncontrolled sexual desire. Part of the salary (penalty) includes:

1. Severe pains during the time of urinating and at other times.
2. Venereal diseases can lead to the discharge of blood instead of urine.
3. They can lead to sterility so that, some day, when you are married, you will find that you cannot have children.
4. They can lead to diseases of the heart.
5. They can lead to diseases of the brain. In fact, a venereal disease such as syphilis can in its final stage attack almost any organ in the human body.
6. They can lead to impotence.

I will never forget the story of a young man. He came to us from one of our provincial capitals. He had committed fornication with a prostitute once and the salary that he got from that one act was that he contacted a venereal disease that made him impotent. He sat before us waiting for his turn to be prayed for. He was tall, slim, handsome but withdrawn and impotent. He had gone out to enjoy forbidden sex and now the tables had been reversed – he was being enjoyed! By the grace of God, the Lord Jesus healed him, but this solution came after years of utter misery and visits to many hospitals that left him without hope and with empty pockets! So, think about it. Before you commit the next act of fornication, remember that you may in that one act give away your capacity for normal sexual life for all of the future.

Maybe you will not become impotent, but have you thought about the capacity of venereal diseases to make you sterile?

You are perhaps thinking of the day when you will be married and have children of your own. This is good thinking. But what of the fornication you are committing? You are gambling away your opportunity to become a father one day. Young girl, what about you? You may say, "Well, girls do not become impotent from venereal diseases." You are perhaps right. But what of barrenness? Have you considered the fact that, in that one act of fornication to which you may give yourself, you may ruin your possibility of ever becoming a mother? Think about it. Maybe some day, your husband will drive you away from home because you cannot conceive and give birth to a baby. Maybe he will one day bring in a second wife and so cause you heartache because you cannot bear him children due to your life in fornication. Do not say, 'I will do it only once.' One time is enough to land you into deep trouble that will cause you anguish all your life on earth and win you the lake of fire as your everlasting home, where your lust for sex may reach its climax, but never know one second of fulfilment!

Another thing that must be borne in mind is that you can cause another person to become infected with your venereal disease, even though the person has not had any sexual relationship with you. We know that syphilis can be transmitted at some stage through a handshake. Think of the seriousness of it. For a healthy person to become a sufferer because of your sin! Think of the huge sums of money that the government wastes in the treatment of venereal diseases. Is this a justifiable use of our national resources? Is it not obvious that those who abuse sex and get into such problems are an undesirable liability to national resources? Have you ever thought about the fact that your acts of fornication are causing the government money that could have been better used elsewhere?

2. Unwanted Pregnancies

Fornication sometimes results in pregnancy. Because the fornicators are ill-prepared for the consequences of their acts, the babies are often unwanted. First of all, it is obvious that those who engage in fornication cannot enjoy sexual relationships to the extent that God meant them to be enjoyed. One reason for this is fear. Fear of pregnancy venereal disease being discovered in the act or in marriage where, in the case of the woman, the husband would find out that the wife was not a virgin. This fear may mean that those who overcome it and get involved in the act, may develop attitudes that may hinder full sexual enjoyment in the married life. The author knows of cases where women could not fully enter into the sexual life because of guilt from past forbidden experiences. In one case, the husband almost had to literally rape his wife! In all these cases, conversion to Jesus Christ, confession of the sins of the past, and the assurance of God's pardon brought freedom.

Pregnancies that result from fornication can lead to abortion. Abortion is murder, and God will deal with all murderers accordingly. He will deal drastically with four or more classes of people who are involved in the murder of unborn babies:

1. The pregnant girls and women.
2. The boys and men who make them pregnant.
3. The parents, friends, etc, who finance the abortions.
4. The doctors, nurses, medical students, etc, who help the girls to abort.
5. The leaders who pass laws that legalize abortions.
6. The scientists who produce drugs whose sole purpose is to induce abortions.

Think for a moment of that baby that you murdered while it was still in the womb. Would it have been a boy or a girl? How old would he or she have been now? Would he or she have been an important statesman?

- scientist
- spiritual leader
- etc,

and contributed significantly to world affairs? Yet you killed it and gave it no chance! How do you think God thinks about what you did? Do you know the great loss that you have caused the world? Do you know the extent to which you have frustrated the purposes of God?

Abortions also have other repercussions. A senior medical doctor in our national hospital said that in the year 1976, he had ninety-nine cases of criminal abortions brought to his clinic.

Of these, 80 will never give birth again because the way the abortions were carried out damaged the reproductive system in an irreparable way. 6 of the rest died. These are just the salary advances for breaking God's law. To want illegal pleasure and to have it and then to be barren for the rest of your life, cannot be real enjoyment. Can it?

Abortions sometimes lead to deformed bodies. We know of a girl who was somehow twisted, bent, after an abortion. She has never returned to her normal form. Is that enjoying the sexual life?

When the pregnancy is not aborted, the pregnant girl suffers a lot of shame. Imagine that she was slim and straight and doing very well at school. Then because of fornication, her stomach starts to grow and she begins to develop only in one direction! She may begin to sleep in class, miss some classes, pretend and try to hide the exhibits of her secret life. She may fail and leave school, or marry someone she does not love, or someone who is forced to marry her, and then have hell on earth in a bad marriage as salary advance of the real hell that awaits those who disobey the commands of the Lord!

Imagine a child conceived outside wedlock. Sometimes the boy who is responsible refuses to own up. He is not sure. He may not want to identify with the girl anymore. Most boys find pregnant girls embarrassing and ugly and, anyway, they do not want them anymore. They have had all that they could get out of them. Sometimes the girl does not even know who is responsible for the pregnancy!

Imagine a birth certificate that reads something like this:

Father's Name: _

Mother's Name: Y

Would you want to be the bearer of such a birth certificate? How sad!

Imagine another birth certificate that reads something like this:

Father's Name: X

Mother's Name: X

In this case the child is made to appear as the child of the girl's father; as if to say that the father committed incest with his daughter and produced that child.

I am persuaded that you would not want to be one of the children whose birth certificates we have just been talking about. They are bastards. They have very deep problems. Some of the problems are practical. Others are emotional, psychological.

Among the practical problems are:

1. The lack of a home where the child can be brought up. The unwed mother often leaves the child with her parents or grandparents and returns to school. The child is an embarrassment to these parents and, sometimes, they may not have the means to bring it up.

2. Often when the girl later on gets married, the husband may not want the child. When a man brings in children that he had from his fornication in the past, his wife rarely accepts them fully.

Among the psychological problems are:

1. The lack of identity: Such children often lack a sense of belonging. Sometimes they change homes very often in the cause of childhood, and this does not help a child in its development. Does the child belong to the grandmother, uncle, parents of the girl, etc, where it is forced to be brought up? Such a problem often has life-long effects on the child.
2. The lack of security: They feel rejected. They, therefore, tend to be arrogant so as to try and cover up their inferiority and insecurity. They may tend to grab things and cling to them, and all such manifestations of insecurity.
3. The lack of a balanced character: In the eternal purposes of God, children are normally to be brought up by a father and a mother. The father has the responsibility of disciplining the child in major issues, while the mother does the discipline in minor issues. For children born outside of wedlock, they may become spoiled children because the mother tries to give them all they want because she feels guilty for not being able to give them a normal home, or they become hard as a result of the cruel treatment that they receive while struggling to grow up with someone who does not love them.
4. Such children very often become robbers, thieves and leading criminals in one way or the other. They cannot be held solely to blame. Life has been hard on them. They will tend to follow in the footsteps of their parents – produce other bastards; for is the saying not true: "Like father like son"?

When one thinks of the problems that a child who is born as a result of an act of fornication has, what can one say to the ones who are at the root of all these problems - the fornicators? When a boy feels like killing his mother because she cannot show him his father, do you blame only the boy?

Every act of fornication has the potential of bringing one such child to life with all the problems that await it. You who are bent on such acts, have you counted the cost? Have you thought about the future of any child that may be born as a result of that act?

Some may say that contraceptives are now available and so pregnancies can be avoided and fornication will not lead to any unwanted babies. To some extent that is true, but I want you to remember two things. The first one is that by breaking God's law you are in for punishment, whether or not there is a pregnancy. The second one is that contraceptives sometimes do fail. An "accident" may occur and the unwanted pregnancy may then occur. You have no guarantee that by using any method of contraception you can be absolutely sure that no pregnancy will take place, except perhaps by destroying all possibilities of ever having children. In addition, contraceptives bring with them other problems. One of them is the fact that they can ruin your chances of having children, even when you have ceased to use them.

Looking at all the problems that a child who is born outside of proper marriage has to face, can anyone in his proper senses call the act by which such a child is conceived 'enjoying the sexual life'? I do not think so.

3. Impact On Marriage

Fornication has far-reaching consequences on the marriage of all who have been involved in it. We have mentioned the fact that the venereal diseases may cause the couple never to have children in the marriage. I well remember a visit I made to some town. At the beginning of the meeting, a young man came to me, wanting to talk to me. By his side was his young and beautiful wife. I asked him to wait until the meeting was over and then I would listen to him with real concentration. When the meeting was over, he told me his story. He had gone in for the pleasures of forbidden sexual relationships, caught syphilis and, while yet untreated, gotten married to a young girl and passed the disease over to her. They had since then not only failed to have any children in four years of married life, but they were suffering physical torments and all their money had gone on drugs. He was sad and frustrated and so was she. He had gone out to enjoy the sexual life, but was it real enjoyment? Had it lasted? In his case, I turned them over to the Lord Jesus who healed them completely, but they had spent many years in agony that would have been spent in enjoyment had the husband obeyed God's Word from the beginning.

Another consequence of fornication is that, even when no venereal diseases are had, it ruins marriage. Think of a man who "prepares" for marriage by committing fornication with many girls. In his marriage he will need the contribution of each of those girls to be truly fulfilled. How can one woman later satisfy a man who has had experiences with dozens of others? What if his wife lacks the experience that the other women had? What if she is different from them in response? How can one man satisfy a woman who all along life had given herself to say tens of men? How can this miserable man called husband ever fully satisfy such a woman?

All who go in for the sin of fornication, experimenting on men or women, come out of it less prepared to find happiness in marriage.

Another way of looking at it is this: Who wants the remains of over-used property? Say someone bought a car for you and decided to drive it first. He was then involved in one accident in which the left front door was bashed, and then in another accident in which the right front door was bashed, and then in another accident in which the rear was dented, and in another in which the engine was partly damaged, and so forth. After all these accidents, he brought the remains of the car to you as a gift of love. Would you like it?

Many brides and bridegrooms go into marriage over-used, damaged and ruined from many an accident of fornication. Many a man and many a woman say, "I now want to settle down and be married." They are otherwise saying, "I must now look for someone on whom to heap the remains of my broken

- body
- mind
- emotions
- etc,

and they are mad enough to call this one who acts as their garbage heap "my beloved husband" or "my beloved wife," and they invite the rest of a mad world to come and watch a girl who is everything but pure, wear sparkling white and give herself to a man who has spent his life so far giving himself to multitudes of other women and has no intention of stopping.

Has a man no right to expect his wife to be a virgin on the night after their wedding? Has a woman no right to expect him to have had no sexual knowledge of any woman before that night after the wedding when she gives herself to him? Are virgins out of date? Is fornication enjoying the sexual life?

Even when the act of fornication was committed with the one person who later became the partner in marriage, it, nevertheless, leaves scars on the life and marriage. Normally speaking, a man will not look forward to marrying a girl he has already used. He would prefer the one he has not had any sexual relationship with. If the two have already committed the sin of fornication, what more is there to look forward to on that day called "the day of marriage"? A man may feel emotionally more attached to a girl but, because he has already known her sexually, he would prefer another girl whom he has not known sexually for a wife. Most men are like that!

We conclude this section on fornication by saying that fornicators do not only break God's law, they break themselves!

Adultery

Adultery is a sexual relationship between two people one or both of whom are married, but not to each other. Much of what we have said under the heading "FORNICATION" applies here, but there is more to it.

Adultery will earn the same punishment from God as fornication. Most fornicators continue in marriage as adulterers and adulteresses. Once a person has made up his mind to break the law of God before marriage, he will naturally have no constraints to stop after marriage.

The pronouncement, "I declare you husband and wife," do not change the man and woman. Their hearts remain the same and, at the earliest opportunity, they will continue their lives as before. A man who would not control himself before marriage does not suddenly acquire discipline over himself. A woman who went with five men does not by signing a marriage certificate and putting on a diamond ring cease to desire many men. The best way to avoid adultery is to have avoided fornication.

There is the thought that men can commit adultery, but the women must not. This is foolishness, of course, and the number of women who are running wild with adultery is enough to tell the men that their expectations are ill-founded. The man is the head and leader of the home. Is it not only to be expected that his wife should follow his example? One woman told me, "When my husband enters his car and goes out in one direction, I, too, enter my car and go in the opposite direction. If not, I would starve and allow myself to be cheated." May I say to all my readers, "Your partner is most likely doing the same thing that you are doing secretly." Does that make you happy?

The children in a home where one or both parents commit adultery are more likely to commit fornication before marriage, and later on commit adultery in marriage. Even when the parents commit their sins in strict secrecy, they, nevertheless, bear an impact on the children and that will help them go the same way. Two examples from the Bible illustrate this point.

Abraham sinned twice by lying that his wife Sarah was his sister in order to save his skin. Later on his son Isaac committed the same sin by lying that his wife Rebecca was his sister in order to save his skin. David committed adultery secretly with Uriah's wife, Bathsheba. His son Amnon later on committed incest with his sister Tamar secretly, but David's son Absalom committed adultery with David's concubines in the sight of all Israel.

Your children will commit the sins you are committing, and worse ones too!

Some day you will see the sins you are committing being committed by your children to a greater measure than you ever committed them, and then you will face up to the things you do not now want to face.

Are you married but committing adultery? You will one day see a married man use your daughter and ruin her. It is the salary advance that you will reap for your adultery, but that is not all, God will throw you too in the lake of fire for breaking His law. The laws of divine justice demand that you be punished and God will not let you go free.

Homosexuality

Homosexuality includes all sexual relationships between people of the same sex. If a man has a sexual relationship with another man, this is homosexuality, and if a woman has a sexual relationship with another woman, this is a form of homosexuality called lesbianism.

It aches my heart to write on these things, but what can I do? Five years ago, we had to minister God's healing to a religious white man in our country. He had become a homosexual while studying to become a clergyman. By the time that God led him to us so that we might be His instruments of ministry to this man, he had already had sexual relationships with six Cameroonian boys! By the goodness and power of our God, he was set free from this abuse of sex, which had had such power over him that he was more or less a slave. Such an encounter, coupled with rumours of homosexual practices in some schools and in some circles, forces one to face the fact that the trend is developing fast and, some day, we may see a man married legally and religiously to a man on our shores or a woman married legally to a woman, as it is already the practice in some countries overseas.

What is the mind of God on this matter? Let us turn to the Manufacturer's Guide and read what it says. *"For the wrath of God is revealed from heaven against all ungodliness and wickedness of men who by their wickedness suppress the truth… for although they knew God they did not honour him as God or give thanks to him, but they became futile in their thinking and their senseless minds were darkened…. Therefore God gave then up in the lusts of their hearts to impurity, to the dishonouring of their bodies among themselves, because they exchanged the truth about God for a lie and worshipped and served the creature rather than the Creator, who is blessed forever! Amen. For this reason God gave them up to dishonourable passions. Their women exchanged natural relations for unnatural, and the men likewise gave up natural relations with women and were consumed with passion for one another, men committing shameless acts with men and receiving in their own persons the due penalty for their error. And since they did not see fit to acknowledge God, God gave them up to a base mind and to improper conduct. They were filled with all manner of wickedness, evil, covetousness, malice. Full of envy, murder, strife, deceit, malignity, they are gossips, slanderers, haters of God, insolent, haughty, boastful, inventors of evil, disobedient to parents, foolish, faithless, heartless, ruthless. Though they know God's decree that those who do such things deserve to die, they not only do them but approve those who practise them"* (Romans 1:18-32).

SIN IS PROGRESSIVE AND GOD'S JUDGMENT IS ALSO PROGRESSIVE

With regard to homosexuality the Bible shows clearly that sin is progressive, and so is the judgment of God.

Phase One: Sin And Judgment

1. They suppressed the truth they knew about God by their wickedness.
2. They did not honour God.
3. They did not thank God.
4. The result of these sins is that
5. They became futile in their thinking.
6. Their senseless minds became darkened.

God judged them by giving them up in the lust of their hearts to normal sexual sins, i.e., impurity, the dishonouring of their bodies among themselves.

Phase Two: Sin And Judgment

The people did not repent. Had they repented, things would have been different. Instead:

7. They exchanged the truth about God for a lie.
8. They worshipped the creature rather than the Creator.
9. They served the creature rather than the Creator.

God then acted in judgment by giving them over to homosexuality which meant that

    a. Their women exchanged natural relationships (with men) for unnatural relationships (with women).

    b. Their men gave up natural relationships with women and were consumed with passion for one another, men committing shameless acts with men.

    c. They (the men and women) received in their own persons the due penalty for their sin.

Phase Three: Sin And Judgment

The people did not repent. They instead did not see it fit to acknowledge God. This was their final sin. And for this God brought in the third phase of judgment. He seemed to say to them, "You are on your own now. Go on as you want."

The Bible says God gave them up to

a) a base mind,

b) improper conduct,

that is manifested in three dimensions:

1. All manners of:
    - a. wickedness
    - b. evil
    - c. covetousness
    - d. malice
2. They are full of:
    - a. envy
    - b. murder

c. strife
   d. deceit
   e. malignity.
3. They are:
   a. gossips
   b. slanderers
   c. haters of God
   d. insolent
   e. haughty
   f. boastful
   g. inventors of evil
   h. disobedient to parents
   i. foolish
   j. faithless
   k. heartless
   l. ruthless.

By these, they manifest the fact that they are already condemned. The Judgment Day will only seal their condemnation.

My dear reader, where are you in this progression?

Are you in phase one?

or phase two?

or phase three, dimension 1?

or phase three, dimension 2?

Please listen, you can repent today and be forgiven. Do not take the next step in the direction of sin. Please I plead with you to turn back and go in the way of repentance.

Other sexual sins are also progressive

All sexual sins are progressive.
1. It may begin with a forbidden look.
2. It may then follow with a forbidden visit.
3. Then forbidden words.
4. Then a forbidden touch.
5. Then a forbidden embrace.
6. Then a forbidden kiss.
7. Then a forbidden sexual act.
8. Then a forbidden pregnancy.
9. Then pretence.
10. Then lying.
11. Then the murder of an unborn baby.

And the reward, the lake of fire.

Let me ask you, "Where are you in the above progression?" Won't you repent at the stage where you are? Please do not move to the next step. The further you go down the ladder of sin, the more difficult it will become for you to retreat.

All sins are progressive:
1. It may begin with laziness.
2. Then continue as covetousness.

3. Then a small theft.
4. Then more theft.
5. Then large-scale theft.
6. Then murder to cover up some theft or to enable some theft to take place.

Again, I ask you a question. It is this: "Where are you in the particular progression of sin which preoccupies you at the moment?" Will you listen to the warning of God and stop? If you stop today, it may prevent a disaster that could ruin many lives on earth and end in the lake of fire.

Will you stop?

Will you stop at once??

Chapter 5

Human Attempts At Solving The Problem

How do you solve the problem of:

1. Young people who are caught up in the sin of petting and the reading of pornographic literature?
2. People bound by the destructive habits of masturbation?
3. People who commit the sin of fornication?
4. People who commit the sin of adultery?
5. People caught up in homosexuality?

How do you solve the problem of people who are bound by guilt because of their sin? What of those with emotional diseases that result from the abuse of sex, children born outside wedlock, unwedded mothers, etc. What of those with physical diseases that have resulted from the abuse of sex, incurable venereal diseases, impotence, sterility, etc. How do you solve the problem of those who want to quit the committing of sexual sins, but find themselves bound by these sins and sinful habits?

How do you solve the problem of people whose past sexual life has ruined their possibilities of ever having an enjoyable sexual life in marriage?

How do you solve the problem of the gap created between God and man through sexual sins? How does the hell-deserving violator of God's law become a citizen of heaven with the full status of a son of God?

Human attempts

Many people tell someone who is caught up in the sin of petting, "Make up your mind and stop petting." They say the same thing to the fornicator, adulterer, the one who masturbates and the homosexual. Now, if it were possible for those who are caught in the chains of these things to heed this advice, it would do some good. However, the problem is that those who are caught up in these things have no power to set themselves free. They are like prisoners bound with chains and who cannot liberate themselves. They may say, "I will stop petting," but their resolve will evaporate when the next opportunity comes up, and back to it they will fall. The same thing will be said by those who masturbate, fornicate, commit adultery, commit homosexuality.

They have the capacity to make decisions, but they have no power to keep them. They are like corpses that say, « I will stop decaying,» but they just continue to decay.

Apart from personal lack of power to accomplish what is willed, there is the pressure of society. I well remember a boy in the High School who went around looking for those boys who were still virgins. When he found some (for some indeed exist) he would give them money and say to them, « Go and get a woman for yourself and prove that you are a man. » Other boys just mocked at those who were still virgins and gave names. Some were described as impotent, eunuchs, and so on, but everything was done to get everyone into the boat of premarital sex. The pressure to have all conform to the standards of those who were already given to premarital sex was so strong that most boys succumbed to the pressures. With such pressures the attempts at not continuing in the way of sin are hardly successful.

What of the past?

Let us take a situation where someone was able to stop the type of abuse of sex in which he was caught up. Let us say, a fornicator was able to stop fornicating, would he then be free? Would his problem be solved? No. It would not really be solved, for there are three problems involved:

1. The problem of the sins of the past that have already been committed. These are there. By his past sins, he has broken God's law. Even if he were to stop breaking God's law today, he would still have to account for God's law that was broken in the past. This is quite obvious. If a thief stole in the past and appeared before a judge and then said to the judge, « Mr. Judge, it is true that I stole that car and that money. However, these were in the past. I have stopped stealing. Set me free. » Would the judge set him free because he has reformed? Certainly not! He must:

    a. Pay for the things stolen in the past
    b. Bear the penalty for those acts of the past.
    c. Be of good behaviour in the future.

The sinner, too, has a debt with God for his past sins. He must be punished for his past sins and HE MUST LIVE ACCORDING TO GOD'S LAW IN THE FUTURE.

2. The problem of the consequences of his past behaviour. What of the children who resulted from his life in fornication in the past and their far-reaching psychological problems? What of the future husband of the girl who can no longer have a virgin for a wife? What of any incurable diseases that were caused by the fornication? What of some homes that were broken because of adultery? What of a man who has become impotent or sterile because of the primary consequences of fornication? If he stops fornication (and the impotent cannot continue any way), does that render him healthy again?

3. The problem of the scars left by these things: He cannot start as a virgin again.

He is like a car that has been in an accident and will bear the marks of that accident all the time.

What of the Future?

Even if the past was well taken care of, what of the future? Would God's law be obeyed in all of the future? Even if the person were by human will power able to stop the physical acts of sin, what about the acts of sins committed in his thoughts? What if he still commits fornication or adultery in his thoughts? Is he not still guilty before God? Certainly he is; for as we saw earlier, Jesus considers sin to have been committed when it is entertained in the heart. No one is able to get sinful thoughts out of his heart on his own. There are beautiful women all around. They arouse desire. A man may be unmoved by one, ten, one hundred, one thousand, but he will meet just one whose appearance will overpower him and he will commit the sin of lusting after her in his heart, even if it is for a short time and, thereby, be guilty before the bar of God. NO HUMAN ATTEMPTS AT SOLVING THE PROBLEM WOULD DO. ALL HUMAN BEINGS HAVE THE PROBLEM TO VARYING DEGREES.

The one who pets with one girl is guilty before God. The one who masturbates once is guilty before God. The one who fornicates with one girl is guilty before God.

The one who commits adultery once is guilty before God.

The one who looks at a woman lustfully once is guilty before God.

The Bible says, *"for whoever keeps the whole law but fails in one point has become guilty of all of it" (James 2 : 10)*. *"Cursed be every one who does not abide by all things written in the book of the law, and do them"* (Galatians 3 : 10).

All human beings are guilty before God. All have committed one sexual sin or the other, at least, in their thoughts. Even if they were 100% without guilt before God about sexual sin (and I do not think that such people exist), they would still be guilty before God because of some other sin.

It could be anger
- lying
- envy
- jealousy
- pride

➤ etc.

It is not sexual sins or any other sin that makes man a sinner. Man is a sinner by nature. Left on his own he will tilt in the direction of sin. All human beings are like that! Sexual sins are only a manifestation, an exhibition, a confirmation of the fact that man has sinned.

The Bible says, *"All men, both Jews and Greeks are under the power of sin, as it is written: None is righteous, no, not one; no one understands, no one seeks for God. All have turned aside, together they have gone wrong; no one does good, not even one"* (Romans 3 : 9-12). *"All have sinned and fall short of the glory of god"* (Romans 3 : 23).

The Bible is not saying that all have practised sin to the same extent. No. That would be untrue. It is not saying that all have turned aside from God to the same extent. No. That, too, would be untrue. The Bible is saying that all have turned away from God to varying degrees at different times. Some have turned away from God by one degree, others by ten degrees, others by fifty degrees, but all have turned away. Some have turned away all the time, others have turned away often, others have turned away occasionally, others have turned away very rarely, but all have turned away at some time or the other, and that makes all sinners.

You are a sinner! You are a sinner!! You are a sinner!!!

If a mango tree bore ten thousand mangoes it would be a mango tree. If it bore only one thousand, what would it be? If it bore even less, let's say ten mangoes, would it not still be a mango tree? What if it bore only one mango?

What if it had no mango fruit on because it was not ripe enough to actively produce fruit, or it was too old to produce fruit? It would under all these conditions still remain a mango tree.

All human beings are sinners, regardless of the extent of their sin. There are no exceptions. In an examination where the pass mark is 100%, those with 99% fail as well as those with 0%. All fail, even though they have all performed differently. In God's examination, the past mark is 100%, that is, perfect sinlessness in motive

> thought
> word
> action.

Anything that is less than that, even by one per cent, is sinful. How high the standard of God is! How sinful all men are!! How hopeless human attempts at solving the problem are!!!

A solution to the human sin problem and its consequences, a solution to the fact that people are not enjoying the sexual life as God really meant it to be enjoyed must be found. If human attempts do not provide a lasting answer, who else can provide the answer? Is there hope for mankind?

Chapter 6

God's Solution To The Problem

God saw that man could not actually solve the problem created by his sin. He saw that man's attempts did not get to the root of the problem. He saw that man's best answer did not satisfy Him whose law was broken by man's abuse of the sexual life. He saw that man on his own could not come back to full sexual enjoyment. He, therefore, designed a solution that was capable of satisfying the following aspects of the problem fully:

1. The anger of God against man who had broken His law.
2. The incapacity of man to free himself from the bondage of sexual sins.
3. The products of the abuse of sex.
4. The need for man to live in freedom from the abuse of sex after he has been set free.
5. The need for a person who had ruined all of the past to begin all over to live as someone who had never messed up his life at all.

The solution of God for the problem is embodied not in any of the following:

- a philosophy
- a creed
- a religious system
- rules and regulations.

God saw that none of these would work. They would not be very different from human attempts at solving the problem.

God's solution is embodied in the

- incarnation
- death
- resurrection and
- enthronement

of the Lord Jesus Christ. We shall look at these very briefly.

THE INCARNATION

When God saw the plight of man, He did not send a solution from a distance. He decided to take human form and come in the Person of the Lord Jesus Christ into the human situation so that He might become the Friend of the sinner. So Jesus Christ took the form of man and was born into the world in order to be the Saviour of the world. The Lord Jesus Christ came into the human situation so that He might bring God into the solution.

THE DEATH OF CHRIST

Jesus did not only come into the human situation. He went to the cross and died for sinners. He poured out His life for the sake of people who are separated from God, because of sexual sins and all the other sins. He poured out His blood on the cross for the sake of sinners. The blood of Christ is available to cover all sinners who turn to Him. When a sinner turns to the Lord Jesus Christ the blood of Jesus immediately covers him from the wrath of God. When the children of Israel were in Egypt, the Lord told them to slaughter a lamb and take some of the blood of the lamb and put it on the two doorposts and on the lintel of their houses. God told them, *"For the Lord will pass through to slay the Egyptians; and when he sees the blood on the lintel and on the two doorposts, the Lord will pass over the door, and will not allow the destroyer to enter your houses to slay you"* (Exodus 12:23). The children of Israel did this and that night the destroyer passed by. He did not destroy anyone in a house that bore the blood marks. But wherever there were no blood marks, the firstborn was killed. Jesus is a kind of Lamb. He shed His blood on the cross for all men. All who turn to Him are sheltered from the anger of God, regardless of the extent or the number of their sexual sins.

In His death, the Lord Jesus took with Him all the records that were written of the sinner's sins to the cross and destroyed them. The truth is that every sexual sin is recorded against the one who commits it. Each

- forbidden
- touch
- kiss
- embrace.

Each immoral thought or look is recorded.

Every sentence of immoral literature read is recorded.

Each look at an immoral picture is recorded.

Each act of masturbation is recorded.

Each act of
- fornication
- adultery
- homosexuality
- lesbianism

is recorded against the person in God's book. All these acts which are a breaking of God's law are on record. None of them is lost. None is forgotten. They are on record so that they will be evidence against the person who committed them on the Judgment Day.

When the Lord Jesus went to the cross to die there for sinners, the Bible says, *"Having cancelled the bond which stood against us with its legal demands; this he set aside, nailing it to the cross"* (Colossians 2:14).

So when a person is in Christ, all the penalty for all his sins - past, present and future - is cancelled once and for all in the death of Christ, and God looks at such a one as if he had never sinned.

When Jesus went to the cross, He took all the sinners with Him to that cruel cross, and when He died, they, too, died. Because they died with Him, they are potentially free from all the consequences of the sins they had committed. This potential becomes a reality when they turn to Christ and acknowledge His death as for them and as theirs. This is only fair, for if a person commits a grave crime, he will be brought to judgment before men when he is alive. When he dies, he can no longer be brought to judgment before men. Death has set him free from judgment for his sin.

In the same way, a sinner who has taken his position in Christ is considered by God as having died with Christ. He is, therefore, free before God from all the consequences of all his past sin. God will never call on anyone who is in Christ to render account before Him for any sexual sin or any other sin that he ever committed. Those who are in Christ are totally free before God from the penalty and consequences of all their sins. Yes, they are free - truly free. Why can God not punish them for their sins? He cannot punish them for their sins because as they have identified themselves with Christ in His death, God considers them dead and, therefore, will not punish a "dead man." Looking at it from a different direction, God punished Christ in the place of the sinner. He cannot punish the sinner again; for this would mean that he is being punished twice for the same offence.

So in the death of Christ, the anger of God against those who have broken His law through sexual sins, and who identify with the Lord Jesus in His death and are thus put by God into Christ, is settled once and for all. God does not look at such people who are in Christ as the fornicators, adulterers, etc, that they were. He looks at them as people in Christ with the holiness of Christ on them. What a wonderful position to be in! You can enter into this wonderful position today!!

The resurrection of christ

Jesus did not only die on the cross. He was buried and He rose again from the dead. He is alive. When a person is in Christ he, too, is made a partner of the resurrection of the Lord Jesus Christ. In his new life, he puts on the Lord Jesus Christ. The power of the Lord Jesus Christ is thus available to all who are in Him to be free from bondage to sexual sins.

This means that a person in Christ has Christ's power available to him and at work in him. Whereas he was bound before by lust, he is now free from the bondage and has power to be pure. This power, the power of the Lord Jesus Christ in those believers who share His resurrection with Him, enable them to live "naturally" free from lust. Their minds, which were sometimes filled with sin and sinful desires, are now filled with the Spirit of Christ and holy desires.

This power of the resurrection life of the Lord Jesus Christ at work in him keeps him from returning to the ways of the past. When he is tempted, the Spirit of Christ within him enables him to overcome the temptation. The desires of Christ take his whole heart in such a way that a man who was once bound by lust and unable to resist any beautiful girl will, while in Christ, see a beautiful girl and instead of lust filling his heart, prayer will build up in his heart and he will pray for her in the following way: «Lord, thank you for this beautiful girl. Help her so that her beauty may not lead her into sin.»

You, too, can share in this glorious resurrection life in Christ Jesus if you will come to Him today.

THE ENTHRONEMENT OF CHRIST

After His resurrection, the Lord Jesus Christ was enthroned at the right hand of God. The Bible, in talking about this, says, *"...according to the working of his great might which he accomplished in Christ when he raised him from the dead and made him sit at his right hand in the heavenly places, far above all rule and authority and power and dominion, and above every name that is named, not only in this age but also in that which is to come; and he has put all things under his feet and made him the head over all things for the church, which is his body, the fullness of him who fills all in all"* (Ephesians 1:19-23).

God did not enthrone only the Christ. He enthroned all who are in Christ. The Bible says, *"But God, who is rich in mercy, out of the great love with which he loved us, even when we were dead through our trespasses, made us alive together with Christ (by grace you have been saved) and raised us up with him and made us sit with him in the heavenly places in Christ"* (Ephesians 2:4-6).

You see, all is tied up with Christ. All who are in Christ enter into the glorious inheritance of Christ. All who are in the devil enter into all the punishment that is the devil's lot.

Those who are in Christ also sit with Christ in the heavenly places far above

- all rule
- all authority
- all power
- all dominion
- every name that is named in this age
- the age to come.

Those who are in Christ are on the throne with Him, so that God has put all things under their feet and made them head over all things.

This is the position of all who are in Christ. By virtue of their exaltation with Christ, they are above the devil, and have authority over him. The devil and all his host and temptation are under the feet of those who are in Christ.

> Fornication has no power over them.
> Impure thoughts have no power over them.
> All sexual sins have no power over them.
> No sin whatsoever has any power over them.
> No temptation has any power over them.
> No relationship of the past has any power over them.

They have power to bring all relationships of the past to an end, regardless of how powerful those relationships were. They are in control. What they could not do by the power of personal effort

strong will

discipline in human power, etc,

they are able to do with the power of the Lord that resides in them and with the authority that comes from their exalted position. They can say to the devil, « Satan, stand still, » and he will obey. He may not like to obey, but he will be forced to obey by the power that resides in their exalted position.

Think of it in this way. A traffic policeman may be small in stature and on his own have no authority. However, when on duty, he is vested with all the authority of the nation, so much that when he raises his hand all vehicles stop. It may be one vehicle or it may be one hundred vehicles. It may be small two-door cars or big Mercedes 600. Each of these vehicles could rush and kill him, but it dare not because the authority of the nation is behind the policeman. The vehicle drivers may not want to wait, but they have no choice. They must wait. By virtue of his authority, he can keep the vehicles waiting for

- one minute,
- ten minutes,
- one hour, etc.

He decides.

He is not answerable to the drivers. He is answerable only to his commanding officer.

The same thing is true of the one who is in Christ. He has authority over all the works of the devil and over all the works of the flesh and over all the world. He needs only to speak and he will be obeyed. Any passion that rises in his heart will obey him. The devil may not want to obey, but he obeys. The one who is in Christ is not answerable to

- the flesh,
- the world,
- the devil.

He is answerable to the Lord with whom he is seated on the throne and with whom he is joint commander.

With this authority, he sets himself free from all that comes upon him as a consequence of his sexual sins. He frees himself from guilt. In the name of Jesus, he receives healing from incurable venereal diseases. In the name of Jesus, he is set free from impotence, barrenness, and all the like.

With the authority of Jesus, he sets the children who were born outside wedlock free from all the associated psychological and other problems which became theirs as a result of their abnormal beginnings. In addition to their authority being used to free people from all kinds of emotional problems, the Lord Jesus actually ministers healing to them. This is also associated with His death on the cross. The Bible says about Jesus:

"Surely he has borne our griefs and carried our sorrows; yet we esteemed him stricken, smitten by God, and afflicted. But he was wounded for our transgressions, he was bruised for our iniquities; upon him was the chastisement that made us whole, and with his stripes we are healed" (Isaiah 53:4-5).

Because He bore the griefs of the whole world, He also bore the griefs of all illegitimate children. He carried their sorrows. He was wounded for our transgressions and bruised for the iniquities of all and with His stripes all who are in Him are healed of the following kinds of diseases:

1. physical diseases,
2. psychological diseases,
3. emotional disorders,
4. inferiority complexes,
5. superiority complexes,
6. etc.

Jesus heals from all diseases so that no trace remains to tell the story. He takes away deep hurts and all the scars left by the sins that were committed and, in this way, restores the person to all that God meant him to be.

The result of this is a new brand of people who are so liberated and restored that no one can read their past from their lives and character, for the Lord Jesus Christ also heals character diseases. For example, girls who were hard, harsh and bitter through maltreatment by men are rendered tender, sweet and loving by the character Physician Jesus. He does not only heal them but He gives them the power and authority to go and heal others in His name.

What of people who had wasted their emotions through loose living by giving

5% to A

2% to B

10% to C

1% to D

etc,

so much that they had nothing left to give? The Lord Jesus restores them completely. In Him, they enter into all the fullness of emotions. The Lord starts with them all over, so that after they are in Him, they are intact emotionally, filled to overflowing, with a capacity to pour themselves out of the command of Jesus to Christ-approved people. They are not only filled and able to pour themselves out, those people who are in Christ have reservoirs of love built into them by the Lord Jesus Christ, so that as they pour themselves out in selfless giving to others, they are refilled. The Lord Jesus told the Samaritan woman who had spent all of herself in a futile search for satisfaction in men, *"Every one who drinks of this water will thirst again, but whoever drinks of the water that I shall give him will never thirst; the water that I shall give him will become in him a spring water welling up to eternal life"* (John 4:13-14). Do you see it? Those who are in Christ receive from Him a spring of love, peace, joy, fullness, etc, that wells up endlessly unto eternal life and unto eternity. This is God's wonderful gift for former sexual perverts and all the other sinners who find themselves in Christ.

The following are some testimonies of people who have actually experienced what we are writing about:

Chapter 7

Examples Of God's Solution To The Problem

Forgiven and healed!

"It was in the month of October, 1977, that this wonderful story began, when in my life of debauchery I met Claudine who is today my charming wife in the Lord Jesus Christ.

At that time, I was affianced to a young girl from my village for whom I really had no deep love that could lead to marriage, but I was resigned to marry her out of duty to my parents. Besides, apart from temporary relationships that I had with girls here and there, I was involved in a serious concubinage with a young woman called Pauline. But the coming of Claudine into my life caused surprising behaviour in me. It was more than mere adventure.

With her, everything was different. Very spontaneously we developed such respect and esteem one for the other that at a certain time, without any previous agreement we began to live like real fiancés, just by silent agreement. Of course, she did not know about my other relationships.

After some time we made one step further in this relationship by deciding to have a child together. Surprised why we hadn't had a child all that while we went for consultation in one clinic in town, which I knew very well for having been there several times before. Indeed, several times I had been a victim of these dirty venereal diseases which one so often catches as a result of indiscriminate sexual relationships so characteristic of our towns.

In such cases, rather than going to queue up in the rare public health centres where negligence, indiscretion and humiliation were the rule, I preferred to spend my small student's allowance in this clinic where consultation, lab analysis and treatment, although expensive, were reliable.

Unfortunately, all these precautions were each time rendered useless, for shortly afterwards, while I was still following treatment, I still fell back into the same trap, at times with the same girl who had contaminated me. All this happened in spite of my many resolutions to keep myself under control. I had become a real slave to sexual desires.

All the same, Claudine and I went to the said clinic and after a certain number of medical tests, the doctor made us understand that our chances of having a child were very slim for the simple fact that I had 'Oligospermie severe,' which he told us meant that the number of spermatozoa present in one milligram of sperm was too small to ensure normal fertilisation. He explained to us that the average density of this is usually 60 million per milligram in man. But I only had 5 million per milligram.

Seeing our disappointment he tried to reassure us by saying that all was not lost, for it was possible to rescue the situation, but only after a long and costly treatment which would demand from us a lot of patience.

I was in the soup. That's where foolishness had landed me. Here I was, ruined, threatened with sterility for the rest of my life. It was difficult for me to accept it. I asked Claudine if she could still accept me like that. Of course, she said, "Yes." I knew she loved me very much, but I could not rely on her answer, neither could I imagine for one moment how our life together could be under such conditions. The shock was too great for me to bear. Finally, I proposed to Claudine that we should separate, but she refused, and we continued our life together.

During the long holidays of 1978, both of us went to my village to spend the holidays. It was her very first time of meeting my parents. But they received her with great joy and, as such, we spent a wonderful holiday. Yet how great was our shock when on our return to town we received a letter from my mother in which she related the comments of the villagers about us! She said that usually, when someone goes to the village with his wife after having been away for a long time, as was my case, he brings along with him all the children that he had had all this while. Curiously enough, in my case, instead of children, we had brought suitcases. (We had only taken along two, Claudine's and mine.)

This letter to me was like a knife cutting through a sore. I did not begrudge those who spoke such wicked things against us, but instead my mother who transmitted them to us. For I did not doubt for one moment that she had simply taken cover behind rumours to tell me what she felt in the depth of her being. Even here in Yaounde, several of those who knew us intimately asked us what we were waiting for to have a baby, but we told them that we did not yet need one.

This situation continued until February, 1979, when came the event that was going to affect our whole lives, not only in the present age, but even more so in eternity. Indeed, in circumstances that are impossible to be forgotten nor left out here, for fear of masking the glory of the grace of God towards us, we each received the Lord Jesus Christ into our lives as personal Saviour and Lord. This is how it all happened:

In spite of my rather religious past I knew deep down within me that I did not have peace with God. Obviously, I proclaimed myself a Christian because I had been baptized right from childhood after having been found capable of fluently reciting in Ewondo some passages of the catechism, which I didn't even understand. After that I was confirmed. Meanwhile, the testimony of my life, which comes through in all that I have said above, was the exact opposite of what I pretended to be. It was as if the more I grew up, the more I was confirmed in sin, so much that I ended up cumulating in me alone all the three great vices that are said to be very difficult to resist, namely: wine, women and cigarettes.

In addition, my heart manifested such great corruption that it was very difficult for anyone to imagine what a viper I really was, so advanced was I in the art of dissimulating my abominations such as jealousy, hatred, hypocrisy, pride, lust and the other sins. I, therefore, knew that with all these I could not commune with a holy God who looks deep down into the heart. I decided quite early to withdraw from all religious activities, having realized that this was playing comedy with oneself. This decision, however, did not bring me the peace I needed with God. I felt His judgment and His anger weighing on me. I was afraid of Him. I tried several times to repress this feeling in me, trying to persuade myself that the God problem was only an idea, an argument which I supported relentlessly each time the occasion arose. But, curiously enough, even when I happened to win in such an argument, I had no peace in my heart.

In 1976, in the search for something to belong to, which would fill the emptiness in me caused by my breaking with my childhood religion, I joined the University Bible Group called the G.B.U, a movement whose aim was to encourage Bible reading among the students. This adhesion did not lead me far either. At most it gave me the opportunity to make my first contact with the Bible, this sacred book which I had until then believed to be the monopoly of only the initiated members of my denomination.

The reading of the Bible only confirmed the feeling that I already had – that I was a lost sinner separated from God. But one question kept arising in me: "What can I do to rid myself of all these sins in which I am so miserably entangled?" I had tried several times by myself to abandon them by the exercise of my own will-power, but I had always failed woefully.

This warfare continued thus until 10th February, 1979, when, to the greatest shock of everyone, we heard the sad news of the accidental death of my closest school friend who was sharing one of the rooms on our campus with me that year. God used this physical death to awaken me from the deep spiritual death in which I had always been.

I suddenly realized the vanity and frailty of this life. I then understood that I could have well been in the place of this dear friend who was just as young, intelligent, and ambitious as myself. What could I have done then if I had suddenly found myself before God without any preparation, with all my sins unforgiven? This question was quite pressing and required an answer, and I could no longer dare to suppress it.

During the moments of reflection that followed this sad event, I was pushed to read two small books which I had bought in the "G.B.U," and which I had left lying about in my room without ever reading them. These books were:-

1. "The way of Eternal Life" by Gordon Lindsay.

2. "God's Love and Forgiveness" by Z.T. Fomum.

God used these books to reveal His inestimable love for me. In them I found answers to most of the questions I had since been asking myself, and to which no one had given me any answer until that day. I understood clearly that God had always loved me and still loved me in spite of my sins. That His Son Jesus Christ, in dying on the cross for my sins, was the proof of this love, and that God was, therefore, only waiting that I should receive His Son now risen from the dead and alive, who alone was able to forgive me and liberate me from all these sins which were imprisoning me, and from which I was incapable of setting myself free.

I could not resist such love. There, alone in this room which used to belong to the two of us, my late friend and myself, I knelt down and confessed all my sins which I could remember, imploring Him to forgive me. Then I invited His Son to come and live in me. I cannot describe the immense joy, the deep peace that took hold of me then, or the feeling of liberation which I felt after that, at the very thought that I was now reconciled with God.

At the earliest opportunity, I ran to Claudine and gave her a copy of "God's Love and Forgiveness," recommending it and insisting that she should read it very attentively. Next, moved by a strange courage which I had never known until then, I went to my first fiancée, told her the whole truth, and begged her to forgive me and to consider that it was all finished between the two of us.

A few days later, when I visited Claudine, she announced to me that she had finished reading the book which I had left with her, and that, touched by God's love, she had resolved to repent of her sins and received Jesus Christ in her heart. With tears in her eyes she told me how she had always been unfaithful to me for all the time we had lived together. It was horrible and unbelievable, for I could never have imagined that of her. On thinking about it today, I am amazed at the instant and radical transformation that Jesus is able to bring about, even in the life of a young believer; for I still wonder what held me back from wringing her neck in that room where we were just the two of us, were it not for Him. Finally, I decided to forgive her by the grace of God. In spite of the pain and humiliation burning in my heart, the love of Jesus triumphed. Today I bless Him and sincerely confess that I am perfectly healed of all these wounds.

After these upsetting events we decided once again to start all over and go on together in our new life. She told me that as soon as she had believed she had written to the author of the book, thanks to the address which was indicated in it, in order to narrate to him all that she had just confessed to me, and to seek his advice.

Out of ignorance of the fact that the normal consequence of our conversion should have been an immediate severing of our illegal union, we continued (How sad!) to cohabit like husband and wife, consoling ourselves that God certainly ought to understand that we had sincerely decided to get married to each other. Alas! We are today deeply regretting this state of things, at the thought of which we cannot but blush.

We continued our consultation at the clinic, but to our greatest disappointment, the situation, instead of improving, only got worse. Not only had the «Oligospermie» persisted, but added to it at present was «asthenospermie modérée,» that is, a malformation of the sperm cells, which already were insufficient.

Concerning our new life with Jesus Christ as Master, the most interesting thing to note is that despite the almost total lack of spiritual assistance of which we were greatly in need, the Lord was taking care of us. One of the most evident fruits of His work in us was the sudden birth of love for His Word and other Christian literature which we could easily get at the « G.B.U. » That is how we came to read two important books on prayer:

1. "Prayer" by J. R. Rice.

2. "Prayer that moves mountains" by Gordon Lindsay.

Through these books the Lord revealed to us His faithfulness in answering prayers. Also, through the reading of the Bible, God also opened our eyes to cases of barrenness that He had miraculously healed. Precisely, in the story of Zachariah told in the Gospel according to Saint Luke, the Lord Jesus incited us to consider attentively verses 36 and 37 of the first chapter, through which He strengthened our hearts and encouraged us to, in faith, get hold of this truth that "Nothing is impossible with God." What He had done for Zachariah and Elizabeth, He could equally do for us.

We, therefore, hung to this truth and we lifted up our cry to the Lord, begging Him to heal me and to remove our disgrace in the eyes of men. We told Him of my mother's mockeries and reminded Him that in His Word, He declares that whoever confides in Him will not be put to shame.

Convinced (I'll never be able to explain how) that God was going to do something, we together agreed that I should stop the treatment that I was following, although the last medical examination dated 18th July, 1979, had shown that the density, instead of rising, had rather reduced to 4.9 million per milligram.

In the month of December, 1979, the reply to the letter which Claudine had written to the Spiritual Adviser after her conversion finally reached us. In his reply, the Spiritual Adviser, after assuring her of God's total forgiveness, arranged an appointment with her, which she actually respected. That is how our Lord led us and integrated us into a community of true children of God who love Him and serve Him with fear and trembling. In a very short time these dear brothers turned out to be a great blessing to us, and the Lord used them wonderfully, as He still does today, in order to consolidate us in Him.

In February, 1980, we were led to obey the command of water baptism such as the Lord Jesus had Himself commanded in His Word. Immediately after that, we had to regularize our situation before God. We were told to repent very deeply of all the impure life which we had lived up to then in illegal union. In doing this we had to prove our sincerity by staying apart from each other until our marriage, if it was the will of God that we be married. We gladly obeyed this from February, 1980 to April, 1980, the actual date of our marriage.

But how blessed we were by this indispensable separation! I will never cease to thank my Saviour for this period of separation, without which our home would never have been what it is today. It is a great testimony which I often use against Satan during difficult moments, reminding him that the Claudine whom I received from God on 19th April, 1980, was totally different from his whom I had met in 1977. Between these two persons was the deep gap between February and April, 1980.

Our marriage was celebrated with great simplicity due to our limited resources, but the Lord Jesus Christ was highly glorified. All our needs for the occasion were provided by our beloved brethren in Christ. We shall live to be grateful to them.

We did not receive any special present on the occasion of our marriage, but deeply convinced that the Lord Jesus had been glorified and perfectly satisfied, we expected to receive from Him a special parcel as a wedding present. In reality this did not delay, for between May ending and early June, 1980, we were already certain that Claudine was expecting a baby. Glory be to God!

A few months afterwards, 25th February, 1981, we received this wonderful gift from God in extremely miraculous circumstances in which God had to intervene sovereignly to prevent Satan from interfering with the aim of depriving us of His blessing.

We named the child Danielle, and the God of Zachariah and Elizabeth also became our God. The birth of Danielle was not simply a happy accident as some wicked tongues would say. Today, 7th September, 1983, Claudine and I constitute a happy home, enjoying perfect happiness in our glorious Lord Jesus Christ.

We have two pretty children: Danielle, and Stephen, who was born on 28th June, 1982. In addition to that we are still expecting another child in December, 1983, which signifies that we have been receiving a child from God each year, in such a way that we are now pleading with God to discipline us a bit. We are infinitely grateful to Him. May all the glory be to Him forever!

Joseph ATEBALENTJA,

Agricultural Research Officer,

Ministry of Higher Education

And Scientific Research,

Yaounde.

I am so changed

I count it a privilege to make it known that Jesus is alive and that He not only changes lives, but gives eternal life to all who invite Him into their hearts. He did what religion and all else did not succeed in doing in my life.

Before I invited Jesus to become the Lord and Master of my life, I lived for myself. Certain circumstances in my life, which I am going to relate here, will make this clear: the fact that I was a sinner.

First of all, I easily got angry. It was as if I was bound by this sin, because it just controlled my life. Consequently, I could fight easily with anyone who made me angry. When I was angry, I did not care if my opponent was stronger than I. While I was doing my last year in Saker Baptist College, Limbe, I was made a perfect in charge of a dormitory of twenty-two girls. One night, when we were about to sleep, I noticed that there was no drinking water. I sent out the girls who were responsible for drinking water to go and bring water that night. On their way to the tap, they met the Principal and he told them to return to the dormitory and to fetch water the following day. I was not only angry but proud and, as such, when they came back, I sent them back to go and fetch the water. I had no respect for the Principal, for I yielded to the anger which always controlled me. These girls were finally brought back to the dormitory by the Principal himself.

Three years later, after I had left the High School, I was looking for a job. During this time I knew frustration as never before. I thought I could do away with this by going to the cinema. I made sure I saved the least franc I could get so as to go to the cinema. I became so used to the films that while watching the films, I could easily narrate to someone sitting by me how the film was going to proceed, even though I had never watched that particular film before. This was because I had become so used to watching them that I could imagine what would appear next on the screen. I watched all sorts of immoral and horrible films, hoping to drown my frustration.

However, the frustration continued. Soon there was an evangelistic crusade on the Bamenda Stadium organised by believers. This campaign lasted ten days, but I went there only on the last day because I heard that people were crying over their sins. After the gospel was preached, the preacher asked that those who recognized that they were sinners and wanted Jesus to forgive them and come into their hearts, should indicate. I did so and I was prayed for. The preacher also asked that those who were sick and wanted Jesus to heal them should indicate. I had chronic filaria which gave me black spots on my leg. For some years, I had followed medical treatment but was not cured. So, that night of the campaign I indicated and prayed to the Lord Jesus. The preacher also prayed for us. Some days later, I noticed that my filaria and black spots were gone and have been gone ever since.

However, when I returned home I never went to the meetings of believers so that I could be taught and helped to grow in the faith. I also did not really understand what it meant to give one's life to Jesus and, consequently, I went back to my old life in sin. Afterwards, I left Bamenda for Yaounde in search of a job and some months later I returned to Bamenda and was hospitalised. I was sick. I was sick with the salary advance of sin. I had committed an abortion. I had become a criminal. While there in the hospital, I was almost dying. For once I opened my eyes as I was lying down on the hospital bed and saw a lot of people surrounding my bed. I don't know what happened. During my stay in the hospital, there was a nurse who visited our ward and while she gave treatment to the patients, she sang a particular song, and this she did for two days. This song, as I realize now was a message to me.

Life without Christ is full of problems

It's full of problems

But when you come to Jesus right now

Problems will go away.

Life without Christ is full of misery

It's full of misery

But when you come to Jesus right now

Misery will go away.

I heard the song, but it had no influence on me because my heart was already made up that if I left the hospital, I was going to give my heart to God, to live for Him. I soon left the hospital and was given my hospital book in which was written: "CRIMINAL ABORTIONIST." I came back to Yaounde and started work.

A few days later, I went to the Evangelistic Centre where those believers who had organized the crusade in Bamenda were holding their meetings. My aim of going there was not to hear the gospel preached but rather to ask them what I must do to become part of them, that is, to give my heart to God and to live for Him. However, on that day, the gospel was still preached, after which there was a call for those who wanted to invite Jesus into their hearts to indicate. I indicated, and I prayed, asking Jesus to forgive my sins and to come into my life. The preacher also prayed for us. Jesus did answer my prayer and came into my heart on that day, the 23rd of April, 1979. He changed my life and I have never been the same again.

One of the radical changes Jesus has wrought in me is that He has transformed my heart, which did not know God nor care about Him into one that not only loves Him, but desires Him. More than that, He has set me free from anger. Instead of hating people, bearing grudges and being angry with them, He has made me able to love those who wrong me and also bear with others in their weaknesses. Again, instead of a shy and joyless life full of sin, He has not only filled me with joy, but also with boldness to make known the fact that Jesus is still alive and sets captives free. No more immorality! Jesus has made me able to live in purity. I used to be reserved, being bound by sin, but my chains have fallen off. Jesus did it. In fact, His love is continually taking possession of me, enlarging me and enabling me to give myself away in love and service to others.

In fact, it's impossible to talk about all the changes that Jesus has brought in my life. This is because it is God's very nature dwelling in me now, a totally different nature from what I used to have. I am a new girl. A new girl indeed!! I have just one desire yet unfulfilled. That desire is to have Jesus return and take me to Himself so that I may live with Him forever.

MUSA Ordilia,

Ministry of National Education,

Yaounde.

Saved, healed and truly liberated

There have been two outstanding periods in my life: The first one which ended in 1978, and the next one which began then, is still going on and will never end.

In the first part, that is, from childhood until 1978, I was a slave to sin. This slavery was rather horrible as far as the sexual dimension was concerned.

My sexual life started very early, in fact, too early. At the age of four, even before I went to the kindergarten, I already knew what sex was, and I used to have sexual relationships with my playmates. This state of things was greatly influenced by my elders who unceasingly sustained an immoral atmosphere around me. I, therefore, got contaminated very early, and wherever my playmates and I acted "Papa and Mama," it was for us the opportunity to imitate them even in this area.

My childhood playmates and I hardly missed any opportunity to give vent to our sentiments. The hide and seek game was regularly organized, which provided an atmosphere for this immoral life. At that time we did not know the word incest and, therefore, for us it was sex that knew no bounds. Hence, I grew up with my thoughts and my whole life controlled by my sexual desires.

Later on, when I was in the secondary school, my thoughts were continually turned to sex and I lived in two boarding schools where, not to have a girlfriend or two at a time, was something abnormal. All this while, I was baptized and confirmed and I knew that this immoral life was sin before God.

My life was corrupt to the extent that bringing a girl to my parents' house did not frighten me much, although our custom forbade such a thing. Wherever there was no girl around, it did not disturb me to go to the unpopular living quarters in the different towns where I grew up, to satisfy my desires. In the Lower Sixth Form, a prostitute came to live near my house, and I'd rather not tell you what happened during that school year.

In 1977, I had to leave my parents to continue my studies in the University of Yaounde. This was liberty at last! I was far from my parents and meant to live my life. Some students on holidays had made several comments about the ease with which girls could be got in the «Lycée General Leclerc,» «Lycée Technique,» and in the other schools in the town. Hence, it was with adulterous eyes that I arrived in Yaounde. I was now totally free. My parents were no longer there to supervise me or disturb my movements.

In Yaounde, I found things very pleasant and my small allowance was spent on my sexual life. Things, however, did not always go a hundred per cent well. Venereal diseases came regularly and darkened the record. I don't remember how many times I caught these diseases, but one thing is sure: that I never got completely cured before starting new adventures. I can't remember how many times I went to the « Centre Pasteur » for laboratory analysis. I was a slave bound by my passion for sex. Deep down within me I was disgusted by this life and by these diseases that I had all the time. But what could I do? I was incapable of resisting or controlling myself when I was in front of a beautiful girl; my thoughts would just start to devise a plan to get her, or I would already be imagining her in my bed. I was irresistibly carried away by sex, which directed most of my movements. One other thing which I nearly forgot is that in the Upper Sixth Form, one of my cousins had taught me the technique of masturbation. As such, whenever I had no girl at hand I would masturbate.

The development of my immoral life was also influenced by the fact that I did a lot of reading, and if a novel was not pornographic, I did not read it. My friends and I had a mini library of pornographic books with photos of naked men and women committing atrocities. This pleased us a great deal and I endlessly desired to experience what I read and saw in these bad books. My thoughts, as such, were constantly fed with immorality.

A tragedy occurred in 1978. In July, in front of "Anne Rouge" in Yaounde, I took a "free" woman who transmitted to me a worse venereal disease than any of those that I had had until then. That was wet "Ulcerous Chancre," diagnosed by an eminent professor who is a specialist in venereal diseases. I suffered from this more than you can ever imagine. My suffering was both physical and moral. The moral suffering was harder to bear: the fear of becoming sterile for life, the fear of never having a child. It was horrible. All my few francs went into the treatment of this disease. I looked for false reasons to get money out of my parents in order to treat myself. Despite all this, I was not cured.

Some months later I went to see another doctor, for I was in anguish. He sent me for analyses in one laboratory in town and there I spent a fortune. After this there were yet medical prescriptions to face. After the treatment, healing still did not occur. There was still a small wound which caused me pain.

It was in this state that Jesus chose to speak to me of His love. On the 7th of December, a lady invited me to a Christian's house where, for the first time in life, I knew what the Bible said about my relationship with God. Until then I had been considering myself a Christian because I had been baptized and confirmed. But that evening, I knew that I had gone astray, was lost and fit for the hot lake of fire and sulphur. My sins were uncovered. I could play hide and seek with God no more. I knew myself. He, too, knew my heart. I had been baptized and confirmed, but was lost, far away from God. I could not identify my life with that of Jesus Christ. Jesus had never been a fornicator, yet I was one. None of the things that I had done in the dark could ever be said of Him.

That evening I saw my state for what it was and, by the grace of God, my eyes were opened and I saw God's outstretched hand inviting me to repentance. I accepted the offer. God wanted me to live for Him. A week afterwards, the Lord Jesus Christ came to dwell in my heart. That evening was extraordinary. I had never experienced any such thing before. My conscience was freed. The weight of sin which had always weighed on my conscience was gone. I could not feel it anymore. A sudden joy got hold of me. As I lay there in my bed my whole being bathed in joy. I felt an intense desire to jump and sing aloud. My joy was at its climax.

I fell asleep in that state. The next morning I realized for the first time that I was liberated from the weight of my past. I had peace, deep true peace. That day my friend George came to see me and I told him, "George, I am no longer the man of yesterday. Jesus Christ has transformed me. He has changed my life. I do not want to smoke or do the things we did anymore. You may take the rest of the cigarettes which are on the table."

Was the sex problem solved? Not immediately. On the 22nd of January, 1979, a very beautiful woman, a classmate of mine, gave me a letter in which she confessed her love for me. This woman knew very well that I was sick and that I had chosen to follow Jesus Christ. In spite of my decision, my desire to resist, I still found myself in her bed in the evening, after which I went back home disappointed. I had betrayed Jesus and the confidence He had in me. I was broken in my innermost being, and my wound had opened up again. How dreadful!

The lady was told about how I felt in my spirit, but she was just as weak and incapable of breaking the chains of adultery as myself. So for the six months that followed she was my mistress. During this time I took several resolutions not to go with her anymore, but alas! It was as if heaven was shut to our prayers.

This news got to the Spiritual Adviser of the assembly and he called the lady and myself to his office at Mvog-Ada. That evening, the Spiritual Adviser spoke to us with a lot of love and tenderness. He told us of the love of God for us, of the plan of deliverance that God had for each one of us. His words went right deep into my heart. That evening he told me among other things to pray for all the girls that I shall ever meet, so that God should save them and grant them the grace not to fall into men's traps. And I'd like to confess that this advice has helped me to come out of several difficult situations.

That evening the Spiritual Adviser prayed for me and I knew on the spot that the Lord Jesus had delivered me from adultery and that I could never fall into that sin again.

The lady and I came out of his office together, but for me the nightmare was completely over. I had turned over a new leaf and started a new kind of life as far as sex was concerned.

Since that evening when the Spiritual Adviser prayed for me and I knew that Jesus had delivered me, I have not had any sexual relationships anymore. I have neither masturbated nor had any desire for pornographic books, and so on. The Brethren prayed for me and now I am completely healed of «Ulcerous Chancre,» and I know that I shall have children.

Only Jesus could have delivered me from the sexual sin and of all the other sins. I was a slave, bound by sex and other sins: Jesus Christ, the living Son of God, broke my fetters and set me free. At the time of writing these few lines I want to confess that it is four years since I last had sexual relationships with women and, by the grace of God, I shan't have any before my marriage.

What the Lord Jesus has done in my life, He also wants to do in your life. The question is, "Do you want it?" The Lord Jesus said, *"Truly, truly I say to you, everyone who commits sin is a slave to sin"* (John 8:34). So "if the Son makes you free, you will be free indeed."

NOUWEZEM Samuel Vincent,

B.A. (Geography), Teacher,

YAOUNDE.

I FOUND PEACE, HOPE AND HAPPINESS

I am a girl of 24 and I come from the Littoral Province. Since I was brought up in a large family with a strict religious background, my childhood knew no mishaps. I succeeded in my studies since I had good serious ambitions. I lived a very pious life, although I did not know Jesus Christ for who He is.

My life, however, experienced a critical turning point between 1971 and 1978; the period during which life seemed empty and purposeless to me. Loneliness, bitterness and debauchery became my faithful companions.

Mike Brand was my favourite musician in my dark days. I used to identify myself with him in singing:

"Who will know, yes, who will know?

To make me forget, tell me

My only reason for living

Try to tell me

Who will know, who will know, yes, who will know?"

It was a cry from the depth of my heart but, always, sadness alone answered me.

This crisis had begun on the day when the one whom I had considered as my mother until then told me: "Know from today that I am not your mother. I am just keeping you in my house out of pity." For the first time in my life at 13, in 1972, I wanted to commit suicide, but was prevented from doing so.

I should have easily thought that it was mere wickedness on her part if a certain man whom she had always told us was our uncle had not told me in the presence of a female witness: "I want you to know from today that I am your father, but I cannot tell you now all that happened. I shall wait until you are of age." I received this as a shock, which came to reawaken in me the first wound and I ran into my room to cry out my despair. I did not have courage anymore to say a word to this "uncle" who had become my "father."

My suffering did not end there since a year afterwards, in 1975, when I was on holidays in my mother's village, my grandfather took me aside into his room and began to ask me a lot of questions: "Who are you really? Where and when were you born? I do not recognize you as the real daughter of my daughter and, therefore, I cannot mention you in my will." I thought he was mistaken because of his blindness and I reminded him that I was even born in his village according to what was on my birth certificate. He insisted on proving the contrary and his wife confirmed that my "'mother" was not in the village in 1959 (the supposed year of my birth). This was the last straw that broke the camel's back. This injustice was too much for me.

What had I done to deserve such cruelty? Who would ever tell the truth concerning me? Where could peace be found?

My heart became bitter against my family and I wept constantly. I forgot the good resolutions I had taken in my childhood and plunged into debauchery. I was sure in my heart that joy, peace, and love truly existed somewhere, and that one day I would surely find them, otherwise there would be no reason to continue to live. I never for one moment thought of God as the answer, since nobody had ever told me so.

I tried cigarettes, alcohol, dancing, cinema, and strolling with friends. These seemed to help, but as soon as I came back to the house, the nightmare began all over again.

In the High School my school mates used to mock at me that I was still a virgin at 17, but that was the only treasure I was left with, which really belonged to me; and so I stuck to it jealously. And to quieten the desires that were springing up in me, I started masturbating myself. I really intended to conserve my virginity. None of all these succeeded to heal me morally. And as such, in 1976, I made another attempt at committing suicide, but it still failed.

It was at this period that a friend spoke to me about Jesus Christ the love of God, and the salvation He offered. I began to mock at him because I thought I was a Christian (having been baptized, confirmed, and more so the daughter of an evangelist).

He continued to talk to me about the new life which he had found in Jesus. His letters were an evidence that he was speaking the truth, for I had known him for several years, but I still doubted his sincerity when I felt that he might have just found an indirect way of telling me, "I have found another girl. I don't want you anymore." This thought made me harden my heart the more.

He continued to talk about the love of God for me until 1977. As I read the Bible and the Christian tracts and booklets which he sent to me, I began to understand this truth. I decided to follow Jesus and joined the Bible study group in our school. I really enjoyed this new atmosphere: Bible reading, prayer, singing, sharing, and so on; but I did not yet understand that being a Christian entailed breaking with sin and giving up one's independence from God. That would have been too much for me then. And curiously enough, it was at this period that I had my first sexual experience, which left me empty and unsatisfied, with a feeling of shame and guilt towards God, my parents and myself. I found it impossible to say, "No," to this boy, and run away from him in spite of the desire I had. Who could liberate me?

Several months later, in February, 1978, this situation reached its climax, but wonderfully enough, God's overabundant grace intervened and saved me. In February, 1978 then, I discovered that I was two months pregnant and there was a panic. I sought for help from the one who had made me pregnant, no answer. I turned to a member of the G.B.U. (Bible Group), no answer. In the house, Papa had said: "No bastards in my house."

So nobody really loved me? And my beauty, my studies... What was going to become of me? Was this what life really meant? I felt more lonely, ashamed, disappointed and discouraged than ever. I, therefore, decided to end the damned life. I hoped to find peace in the grave. That's how I reached my third attempt at suicide. This time I succeeded to swallow all my tablets. It was at noon on one Friday.

When, towards 3 p.m. I was dragged to the infirmary to receive emergency treatment, I knew that unless a miracle occurred, it would really be my last day on earth. I begged to be taken back to my bed in the dormitory rather than to my parents' house.

And that Friday evening, on my bed in the High School dormitory, I had the time to think before it was too late. I, at last, realized the vanity of life and the judgment which everyone will have to face after death. I understood at last that I was not ready to meet God and that all that I deserved was everlasting punishment in hell.

That evening on my bed, I cried to God and confessed my sins to Him pleading for His forgiveness and mercy. I also asked Him to prove His love for me by healing me of the pain in which I was. I had an ardent desire in my heart that evening to have assurance that He had forgiven me and, secondly, to receive healing so as to bring up the child and serve God all the rest of my life.

That night I fell into a deep sleep and the next morning I was healed. I was so full of joy! I had at last found the long sought-for peace. I wasn't afraid of the future anymore. My shame and despair had disappeared. Today, my daughter is 5 years old and I serve God with joy.

God is no longer a story to me, but a reality. Through Jesus Christ He has forgiven my sins. Through His Holy Spirit He sustains me from day to day and gives me courage and strength to deny myself and avoid sin.

He has given me a new identity, a new family. He has become the source of my joy and peace. He has given me eternal life. And more than everything else, He loves me and I live for Him.

Contrary to what Mike Brand sang, now I sing,

"I know Him, yes, I know Him,

He who has made me forget my past,

He who has become my reason for living

I tell you today

He can do the same thing for you."

Miss Louise NGO-BAKENEKHE,

C.U.S.S. TS2,

YAOUNDE.

TRULY FREED

Having been born into a very pious Catholic family (my father being the friend of white priests), I had a very calm childhood. Naturally, my parents had me baptized and confirmed, and at the age of ten I took my first communion, the Lord's supper.

In spite of all the praises which the people of my village heaped on me, I knew I wasn't as good as that. I was bound by a great number of sins: I was jealous of my small friends who were often better dressed than I was. One of them even had a bicycle, which I coveted. I was very hypocritical. I stole. I lied. I harboured impure thoughts, and I lusted after girls.

As I grew up, sin progressively manifested itself in me in diverse ways. My hunger for sex became pressing and uncontrollable. I often went to have a nice time with little girls telling them, "Show me your sexual organ and I shall show you mine."

A nurse was posted to the village dispensary which was very near our home. She came to live in our house. By then I was about nine or ten years old. I fell in love with that nurse, who was herself eighteen or nineteen years of age. I had lice in my hair, and in the evening I used to go and sit by her and she would catch the lice for me, exploring my scalp with her fingers, a thing she herself enjoyed doing. Such evenings were wonderful for me. Unhealthy desires were already creeping into my mind. Because in addition to that people called me "handsome boy," I was very encouraged and was eager to grow up so as to enjoy sex.

At the age of thirteen, when I was in form two in the Secondary School, I had my first sexual experience with a girl called Rameline who was about my age. We were neighbours and I often went to sleep with her in the small room which she was sharing with her younger sister of three years of age. I braved the darkness of the night, the barking dogs, and also the risk of being caught by the parents.

All the same, our regular meetings could not satisfy me. I went courting other girls and masturbating myself at times. Soon I could not do without sex. The business was facilitated for me by the fact that some girls approached me first, while others would tease me in one way or the other.

I continued at this rate until the fifth form in the Secondary School. There, it wasn't long before I caught a venereal disease. I became very worried and went to the hospital. The nurse asked me to go and bring my sex partner so we could be treated together. After a lot of pleading, I succeeded to take her there. It was a shameful and humiliating scene in the hospital. People, who were deeply touched, streamed out to see the precious little children that we were.

We received treatment comprised of a series of painful injections and had immediate healing, which enabled us to continue our adventure. A few months later, the girl became pregnant. I became frightened and started avoiding her visits henceforth. I soon decided to break this relationship which had become so dangerous.

In disappointment and misery, poor Bibiane (so she was called) had to go back to her village where she gave birth to a baby boy. My conscience tortured me for a long time about that. I understood that the sex game was dangerous. I longed to end all this and devote myself to my studies, but I could not control myself any longer.

In order to avoid further risks of pregnancy, I became attached to the secretary of the High School, a mother of several children who, in addition to being older than I, was more experienced. With her, I was progressing remarkably in vice and in the search for stronger sensations. It was abominable. My parents could not imagine this of me. I continued to be quoted in the village as a boy of exemplary behaviour. To them I remained the model of calmness, obedience and intelligence.

As I was becoming more and more obsessed, I needed variety. So I got another girl who was younger, and took all the necessary precautions with her. Alas! She became pregnant and her rather influential parents threatened me with imprisonment since their child was a minor. It required great diplomatic gymnastics on the part of my parents in order to calm them. This won me a big reputation as a "Show boy." In the High School we formed a famous group (How sad!) of boys who were young for their class and proud of themselves. And we were engaged in a sort of tacit competition as to which of us could seduce the most beautiful girls of the school and the town. This debauchery was certainly one of the reasons for my failure in the G.C.E. Advanced Levels that year.

My parents, although very religious, appeared to be proud to see me in the company of many girls. Neither my father nor my mother commented on this topic, but their kindness towards my girlfriends clearly betrayed their approval. According to my family morale, a young boy could go out with as many girls as he wanted, provided they were neither his sisters nor married.

I had, therefore, acquired the principle of avoiding married women and my reputation remained intact. The priest who was my father's friend, even wanted me to go into the seminary, but my father had other ambitions for me: to make of me a Senior Divisional Officer or a President of a Law Court in order to take revenge on local authorities for their maltreatment of him. He was quite disappointed later on!

Although I was so bound by sexual desires, pride, lies-telling, jealousy, in short, by sin, I continued to go to the Cathedral. Every Sunday morning I would put on my best attire and go for mass. Even if I went sometimes to show off, once I was in the chapel I made an effort to be sincere with God. Some Saturday afternoons, I went to confess to the priest. Often I would choose a priest who did not know me, for then things would be easier for me, and I did not want to lose face before the Abbot Patrice, who liked me so much, and who was my father's friend.

I enjoyed the Catholic mass very much, these solemn moments in the sumptuous cathedral where music continuously flowed from the gigantic barrel organ. For me it was a celestial atmosphere, which touched me very deeply. The priest usually came in through the back door, dressed in a long white robe with golden red fringes, surrounded by mass boys holding candles. Then a benediction song was tuned and the priest would go towards the pulpit, sprinkling "holy water" on us. I joined the long queue and moved forward slowly with hands joined together on my chest, to go and receive the white, thin and round slice of biscuit on my tongue. After that I came back and sat down in a holy manner to begin reciting some "Hail Marys," while continuing to admire those who were yet on the line – elegantly dressed young boys and girls, old mothers who walked as if they were already in heaven.

In spite of all this, my life was going from bad to worse. I had my G.C.E. Advanced Levels and entered the University of Yaounde. My pride increased and I was proud of the ease with which I seduced girls. My friends really admired me. It wasn't long before I made the third and fourth girl pregnant. My student's allowance of 27,000 frs was essentially spent on expensive clothing. A shirt of 18,000 francs was not inaccessible to me. My motto was: "LIVE IN MY TIME." Life for me was empty since it only led to death. In the Upper Sixth form, the Epicurean Philosophy, which advocates a continuous search for greatest pleasure, had greatly influenced me. I had become obsessed by sexual pleasure. The only thing wrong was the consequences which weighed on my conscience and affected my whole being. I thought of all the bastards and all the venereal diseases which these innumerable relationships with all kinds of girls cost me. I took new resolutions: to avoid small girls and have one steady girl friend.

When I passed into the second year of the University I had to go to England for a year's language training. That's where I reached the climax of my debauchery. Among my classmates at this training there was one who was sharper and more enterprising than all of us. He did not find it as difficult to get adapted as we did. Our studies were only given second place. I got attached to this classmate. We went to strip-tease houses, watched pornographic films, and soon we succeeded in becoming members of a pornographic club with membership cards.

In addition to our student's allowance, we worked in factories in the evening and had a lot of money and, therefore, made the best of our stay there. We were in nightclubs almost every night. On our arrival we had been shocked by the lack of decency in the English youth manifested in the fact that they kissed themselves so lengthily at street corners and at bus stops, but now we were doing the same thing.

In this frantic search for strong sensations, we soon found ourselves doing abominable things in drunken groups. We were no longer satisfied with the routine. Our licentiousness brought us to an upsetting denaturation. At the end of the year I failed my final examinations. That was in 1975. On my way back home I stopped in France for a few days and a friend led me to Figale and to Barbese, prostitution homes in Paris.

When I came back to Cameroon, in spite of all the admirations I received from the friends to whom I told all these "achievements," I knew within myself that the balance sheet had been negative. I had burnt up my money uselessly, broken the hearts of other innocent girls, and had become hardened and indifferent. My feelings had lost their freshness. I felt worn out, disgusted, disappointed, to say the least. I was deeply disappointed, but I tried to put on a different appearance. The brothers and friends who listened to me were burning with desire to go to Europe so as to do the same, but if only they knew the misery within me!

This time I decided to look for nothing but a fiancée. I, therefore, had to "try" a certain numbers of girls. Joselyne was very beautiful and kind, but she was not faithful. It was not worth it. Suzanne was calm and kind, but not so beautiful. I was not happy in her company during outings. It could never work. As for Pully, she was beautiful and even motherly, but not so well-educated. Angele suited me for a while. She was beautiful, and gave me all that I needed, but she had a dirty past. She had gone out with my cousin. Marie Andrée matched with me, but she was not submissive. Nicole was educated, rich and kind, but I did not love her. Other girls like Mai, Jeanne and Doris in whom I was interested had one after the other rejected my offer.

During this 'trial,' some of these girls conceived by me and I helped them to commit abortions. Nicole even miscarried twins. My situation had grown worse since my return from Europe. It was lamentable, and to calm my conscience, I would give excuses such as "I am very unlucky in this life. I am not worse than other boys. It is not my fault if girls find me handsome, and so on."

In 1978, I had left the University and was working. I very much wanted to stop this 'dog' kind of life, discipline myself and lead a respectable life. But I was bound and couldn't do anything in spite of my good resolutions. I was ashamed of myself. I still went to confess my sins to the priest, although only occasionally. I still recited prayers. A girlfriend gave me a book on prayer and religious songs, but all this did not change anything in me. At one moment the thought came into my mind that I was cursed. I drove back this despairing thought. I bought a Bible.

The society was putting pressure on me to get married. My father had become extremely impatient on this topic. I myself was convinced that the only way to find happiness and put order in my life was in marriage. So I decided to stop all sorts of considerations, trust fate, and get married. I introduced a girl to my parents and two years afterwards, I got married. Our marriage was blessed two times: by the Reverend Pastor and by the white priest, who spared neither their time nor their zeal for the success of the ceremony. The feast which followed was grandiose and memorable.

I was at last married. I was 31. I congratulated myself for having finally turned over this heavy and dark page of celibacy, debauchery, lies-telling, murder, in fact, of misery. I entered my new status with optimism, even more so as I loved my wife – a girl well brought-up (her father was a church elder, her mother a deaconess, her grand- father a catechist and her uncle a pastor). She could only be a gift from God. In addition I admired her calmness, her obedience, and her cheerfulness gladdened my heart.

During the first two months, life was sweet. I had at last found happiness. I doubted if one could be happier otherwise. We simply loved each other and were determined to succeed and shame the prophets of doom. In spite of all the temptations I faced, I remained faithful to my wife. But in the third month of our marriage something began to deteriorate irreversibly. The flame of love no longer burnt hot. I began to discover new faults in my wife. Worse still, the faults which I knew her to have before and which I hoped to wipe out persisted. She was negligent, lazy, not enterprising, the house was not clean enough, the kitchen was topsy-turvy, my clothes were not well-ironed, my visitors were not well-received, and all the other faults I could find.

I started comparing her to some other girls whose tender care I had discouraged. She was not as hardworking as Monique or Chantal. She neither had the wit nor the sense of humour of Marie-Claire or Suzanne. She was far from being as sensuous as Sylvie or Doretha. She lacked this and lacked that. I was bored with her. I had made the wrong choice. It was the drama of my life. I needed to divorce her before it was too late. I kept thinking. The atmosphere was becoming more and more gloomy in the house. My most joyful moments were the ones I spent outside, with friends to whom I lied that everything was all right.

To closer friends, however, I confessed that marriage was not worth the trouble. I consulted a friend who was a lawyer and he promised to help me. I thought of taking a second wife. I was now convinced that God had cursed me for my crimes and that I had to start all over again. From time to time my wife and I made an effort to save our marriage from this precocious shipwreck. We made concessions, forgave each other's faults, made peace, forgot the past and started all over again. Yet we still fell even lower almost immediately. It was fatal.

In my office and in town, the temptation increased. One of my former fiancées, the one I had loved most and who was already married, telephoned me for the first time. As we talked she said she wanted to divorce. We both deeply regretted not having married each other. From our complaints and lamentations it was clear that we wanted to start afresh with each other. This disturbed me even more.

Endless plans were drawn up in my head. One Sunday afternoon, while I was at home busy doing I can't remember what, a young woman came in smiling and visibly happy. She gave me an invitation to attend an evangelistic meeting. The programme, which lasted 7 days offered songs, testimonies, films and sketches, all about Jesus Christ and for His glory.

In the campaign room I recognized young people whom I knew. One of them had come to my house three years before on a Sunday evening to talk to me about the love of God and the salvation of man in Jesus Christ. I had called him a fanatic and had even shown him my Bible to prove to him that I was also a Christian and that he had nothing new to tell me. Our meeting had not lasted long because I did not like arguing with shortsighted people.

There I also recognized my former neighbours who had often given me tracts and booklets and who had several times before invited me to their 'church service' as if I didn't have a 'church service.' I also recognized the pastor, for I had met him some weeks before and he had given me a tract entitled: "God Loves You," and had asked me to read the message it contained concerning the love of God in whom he believed. He had said this to me with assurance and had gone away. I was very surprised and impressed. This was not the first tract I was receiving and I knew the story that was contained in these tracts – a story about sin and death which did not interest me anyway. I had never taken time to read it seriously to the end.

In this big wooden building which they called their chapel, everybody seemed to be so happy to have been saved by Jesus, to know God, and to have a place guaranteed in heaven. This made me think. To end each evening the gospel was preached by a 'pastor' whom I found too zealous. Each time at the end of his message he asked all those who wanted to give their lives to Jesus to indicate. I was completely exposed and bare. In front of this holiness, the love and the sacrifice of Jesus Christ the Son of God, which were so clearly presented, all the ugliness of my life came before me in bold characters. I could not pretend anymore. It seemed to me that all this had been specially prepared just for me. All the pretexts that I could give could not hold any longer. I had at last discovered the origin of my troubles and sorrows. It was sin. And the infallible answer was there: Jesus. I then realized that I had fallen low and very low, that I was coming from very far away.

It was, therefore, neither a curse, nor ill-luck, nor fate, but my own rebellion against my Creator that caused my misery. And there was a possibility of reconciliation by the One who had been sent and who had sacrificed Himself for the sin of humanity.

I was present at the campaign each evening. On the sixth day I took a decisive step. I abandoned myself to this Saviour who had given His all for me. In prayer, the very first in my life so to speak, I presented to Him all the dirty stains of my life. I told Him something like this, "Jesus Christ, I have exaggerated the sin business. My own case is too bad, but I beg for Your forgiveness. Change me and help me to live a life pleasing to you." And, by faith, I accepted that He had done it.

On going out of that hall that evening, I was no longer the same. My guilt which had piled up over the years was lifted. My rotten life, which had been riddled with sin, was transformed. My hard, proud and wicked heart was changed and full of joy. The filth of my perversion was washed away.

When I went back home, I announced this news to my wife. She did not seem to understand much about all this, but, instead of rejoicing, she wept bitterly. However, I knew that one day she would discover the truth and see the light. Two months later she, too, opened her heart to Jesus Christ who then became the solid base of our home. At that time we succeeded to start everything afresh (from zero) under the leadership of Jesus. It is simply wonderful. It still happens that problems confront us, but this time we kneel down in front of our bed and pray to Jesus who brings us the answer immediately. Now we are happy in our home. We sing together and we are united by the love of Jesus. Who could have believed it? Yet Jesus has done it out of untold grace. The nightmare has given place to peace, hope and happiness.

May all the glory be to my Saviour and my Lord, now and for ever more!

MBANG a BETSEM Jacques,

Branch Manager,

Sociéte Camerounaise de Banques (S.C.B),

Banso Agency,

Banso, North West Province.

Chapter 8

You Can Become A Virgin Again

It does not matter the degree of sexual sins that a person has gotten into. If the person turns to the Lord and is put into Christ, God carries out many miracles in him that restore him, not just to what he was at the beginning, but to what God meant him to be.

Take, for example, someone who has lost his or her virginity. Outside of Christ, this loss is most permanent. This virginity is lost through sexual experience either in thought or in action. So anyone who has ever carried out a sexual act in his mind is no longer a virgin before God, even if on the physical body the marks of virginity may remain.

When a person is in Christ, God restores all that was lost through sin to the person, so much so that his lost virginity is restored, not only before man but also before God.

It is in this wise that the Bible, in talking of women who are in Christ, puts them in two classes:

the married and

the virgins

instead of the three classes that are found outside of Christ:

the married

the unmarried virgins

the unmarried non-virgins.

In the Lord Jesus, there are no unmarried non-virgins. This is very far-reaching, for it means that you who are reading this can become a virgin even if there have been 100 men or women in your life. It means that you can become a virgin, even if you have been a professional prostitute or a student prostitute or a working-class prostitute. God is prepared to transform you into a virgin and leave no marks to tell of your past story. This is very good news.

GETTING INTO CHRIST

We have said that all these good things are for people who are in Christ. You may be asking the question, "How can I get into Christ so as to enjoy all these things?" The answer is very simple. Christ has done everything that is necessary. He has taken your place and died for you on the cross. He put you into Himself when He died on the cross. He put you into Himself when He was buried. He put you into Himself when He arose from the dead and God put you on the throne with Him when He was enthroned.

From God's point of view, it is all done, but He cannot force that which He has done for you, in Christ, upon you. You must accept it yourself. At this moment, all that Christ did is potentially yours. You are a potential king, sitting on the throne and reigning with Christ. But this potential will only be realized from the moment when you say to Christ: "Lord, You did all this for me. It is wonderful of You to have done it. I am very grateful to You. I want all that You did for me to become mine right now. I take my place in You now and renounce all the deeds of darkness in my life and all the works of sin and Satan. By Your power I take my leave permanently out of Satan's kingdom and enter into Your Kingdom. I receive You as my Saviour, my Lord and my God, and I will obey You in everything at any cost. Thank You that You have now received me and I am in Christ 100%. Amen."

Immediately you are in Christ in this way, all that He did for you becomes yours. You have become God's son and you have all the wealth that is yours in Christ to explore. Make sure that you explore all your inheritance and that you enjoy it to the fullest.

Chapter 9

Enjoying The Sexual Life

We said from the beginning of this book that God is the Creator of sex and the sexual life. We also said that He intended that His children should, in obedience to Him and in accordance with the conditions laid out by Him, have the maximum sexual enjoyment possible.

You may ask yourself, "What must I do to have the maximum sexual enjoyment that is possible?" Here is the answer:

1. Repent of all your activities in the sexual realm that have been carried out against the conditions that the Creator of sex has laid down in the Manufacturer's Guide for the sexual life, that is, the Bible. Repent of all the other sins in your life.

2. Receive the Lord Jesus as your Saviour and Lord and obey Him in all things.

3. Receive healing from Him either directly or indirectly (through believers who have been baptized into the Holy Spirit) for all the diseases that have come upon you directly or indirectly, because of your attempts to enjoy the sexual life in ways that the Lord forbade. These diseases may be physical, mental, psychological, emotional, etc.

4. Find out God's original purpose for marriage.

5. Discover your God-given position in that purpose.
6. Find your God-ordained partner for marriage.
7. Carry out your courtship God's way.
8. Be married God's way.
9. Conduct your marriage as God has laid down in the Bible.

In this way you will have unlimited enjoyment of the sexual life. In fact, you will begin to have a foretaste of heaven on earth!

In this book, 'Enjoying the Premarital Life,' we have concentrated on the first three points here, that is, on points 1, 2 and 3. In the next book entitled: "Enjoying the Choice of Your Marriage Partner," we have treated points 4, 5 and 6, and in the last book in this series, which we have entitled: "Enjoying the Married Life," we have treated the last three of these points, i.e., 7, 8 and 9.

Be sure to read all the three books, for only then will you have a complete picture of what God has in store for you!

God bless you very richly!

Zacharias Tanee Fomum.

Come Now To Jesus

There is a fountain

That flows from Calvary

There is a fountain

That flows from Jesus Christ

Come to the fountain

There is a vast supply

Come to the Saviour

He will satisfy you.

There was a woman

Who gave her life to sin

There was a woman

Who gave her life to men

Then she came to Jesus

And found in Him pardon

Then she came to Jesus

And found in Him freedom.

Then at the feet of Jesus

She left her load of sin

Ran to the village

And bid all come to Him

They came to Jesus

And found in Him their Lord

Gave their lives to Him

And entered into life.

Come now to Jesus

He died to set you free

Come now to Jesus

He's waiting just for you

Bow now before Him

Confess your sin to Him

Tell Him to come in

And live within your heart.

Then you, too, like her

Will prove His great power

As He does in you

What He did in her

Satisfied in Jesus

You'll live your life for Him

Serve Him all the time

Until He comes for you.

25th July, 1983

Very important

If you have not yet received Jesus as your Lord and Saviour, I encourage you to receive Him. Here are some steps to help you,

ADMIT that you are a sinner by nature and by practice and that on your own you are without hope. Tell God you have personally sinned against Him in your thoughts, words and deeds. Confess your sins to Him, one after another in a sincere prayer. Do not leave out any sins that you can remember. Truly turn from your sinful ways and abandon them. If you stole, steal no more. If you have been committing adultery or fornication, stop it. God will not forgive you if you have no desire to stop sinning in all areas of your life, but if you are sincere, He will give you the power to stop sinning.

BELIEVE that Jesus Christ, who is God's Son, is the only Way, the only Truth and the only Life. Jesus said, «*I am the way, the truth and the life; no one comes to the Father, but by me*» (John 14:6). The Bible says, «*For there is one God, and there is one mediator between God and men, the man Christ Jesus, who gave himself as a ransom for all*» (1 Timothy 2:5-6). «*And there is salvation in no one else (apart from Jesus), for there is no other name under heaven given among men by which we must be saved*» (Acts 4:12). «*But to all who received him, who believed in his name, he gave power to become children of God...*» (John 1:12). But,

CONSIDER the cost of following Him. Jesus said that all who follow Him must deny themselves, and this includes selfish financial, social and other interests. He also wants His followers to take up their crosses and follow Him. Are you prepared to abandon your own interests daily for those of Christ? Are you prepared to be led in a new direction by Him? Are you prepared to suffer for Him and die for Him if need be? Jesus will have nothing to do with half-hearted people. His demands are total. He will only receive and forgive those who are prepared to follow Him AT ANY COST. Think about it and count the cost. If you are prepared to follow Him, come what may, then there is something to do.

INVITE Jesus to come into your heart and life. He says, *«Behold I stand at the door and knock. If anyone hears my voice and opens the door (to his heart and life), I will come in to him and eat with him, and he with me «* (Revelation 3:20). Why don't you pray a prayer like the following one or one of your own construction as the Holy Spirit leads ?

> «Lord Jesus, I am a wretched, lost sinner who has sinned in thought, word and deed. Forgive all my sins and cleanse me. Receive me, Saviour and transform me into a child of God. Come into my heart now and give me eternal life right now. I will follow you at all costs, trusting the Holy Spirit to give me all the power I need.»

When you pray this prayer sincerely, Jesus answers at once and justifies you before God and makes you His child.

Please write to me and I will pray for you and help you as you go on with Jesus Christ...

If you have received the Lord Jesus-Christ after reading this book, please write to us at the following addresse :

For Europe :

Editions du Livre Chrétien

4, Rue du Révérend Père Cloarec

92400 Courbevoie

Courriel : editionlivrechretien@gmail.com

True conversion (Mark 10:17-31)

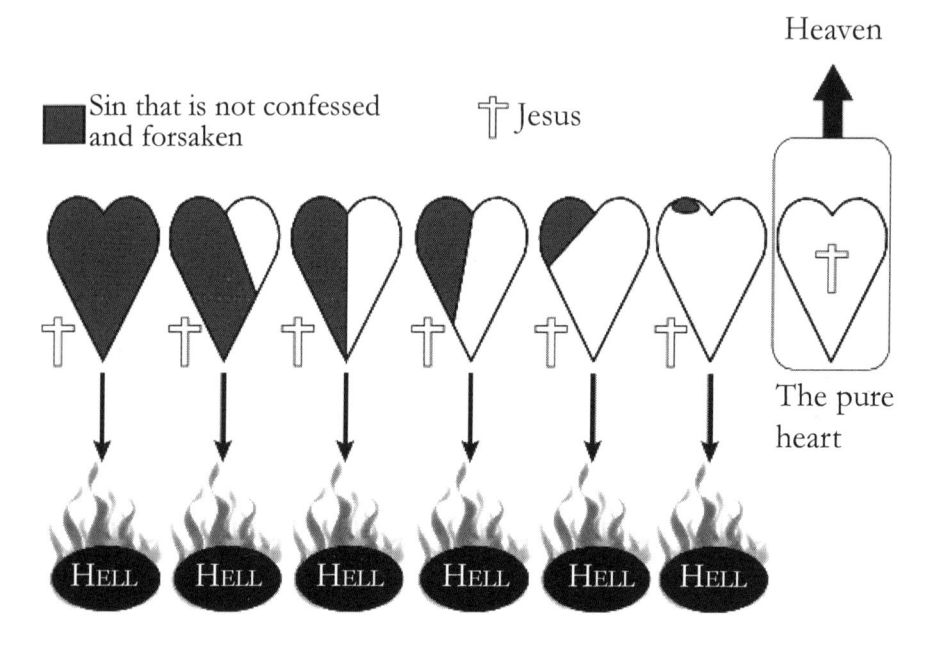

Heaven

■ Sin that is not confessed and forsaken

☦ Jesus

The pure heart

All the blemished hearts represent unsaved persons. The last pure heart alone represents the saved person.

Jesus cannot come in to blot out some of a person's sins and not others. He comes in to blot out all sins or no sin at all.

He blots out sin that is confessed and forsaken forever.

He comes in to be Saviour, Lord and King in all things and in all circumstances or He does not come in at all.

He cannot come in to be Saviour without being Lord and King because He cannot divide Himself. He is Saviour, Lord and King of all or Saviour, Lord and King of nothing at all.

Professor Zacharias Tanee Fomum

About the author

Professor Z.T. Fomum was born in 1945 in Cameroon and was taken to be with the Lord on the 14th March 2009. He was admitted to the Bachelor of Science degree, graduating as a prize-winning student from Fourah Bay College in the University of Sierra Leone. His research in Organic Chemistry earned him a Ph.D. degree in the University of Makerere, Kampala, Uganda. Recently, his published scientific work was evaluated and found to be of high distinction, earning him the award of a Doctor of Science degree from the University of Durham in Great Britain. As a Professor of Organic Chemistry in the University of Yaoundé I, Cameroon, he supervised and co-supervised more than 100 Master's and Doctoral degree theses. He published with others over 160 scientific articles in leading international journals.

The author read over 1350 books on the Christian Faith and wrote over 150 titles to advance the Gospel of Christ. 4 million copies of these books are in circulation in 11 languages, as well as 16 million gospel tracts in 17 languages. In pursuance of the purpose to proclaim the Gospel of Jesus Christ, he also made a total of over 700 missionary journeys in Cameroon and over 500 in 70 nations. These ranged from 2 days to 6 weeks in all the world's six continents.

The author led a Church-planting and missionary-sending movement, by whose ministrations, more than 10,000 healing miracles were performed by God in answer to prayer in the name of Jesus. These miracles include instant healings of; headaches, cancers, HIV/AIDS, blindness, deafness, dumbness, paralysis, madness and diverse diseases.

The author was married to Prisca Zei Fomum and they had 7 children who are all actively involved in serving the Lord. Prisca is a national and international minister specialising in the winning and discipling of children to Jesus Christ. She also communicates and imparts the vision of the ministry to children, with a view to raise and build up ministers for them.

The author owed all that he was and all that God had done in him and through him, to the unmerited favours and blessings of God and to his world wide army of friends and co-workers. He considered himself nothing without them and the blessings of God, and would have amounted to nothing but for them.

May the Lord receive all the glory!

Others Books by Zacharias Tanee Fomum

- THE CHRISTIAN WAY
- The way of life
- The way of obedience
- The way of discipleship
- The way of sanctification
- The way of Christian character
- The way of spiritual power
- The way of Christian service
- The way of spiritual warfare
- The way of overcomers
- The way of suffering for Christ
- The way of spiritual encouragement
- The way of loving the Lord
- The way of victorious praying
-

- THE PRAYER
- The ministry of fasting
- The art of intercession
- The practice of intercession
- Praying with power
- Practical spiritual warfare through prayer
- Moving God through prayer
- The ministry of praise and thanksgiving
- Waiting on the Lord in prayer
- The ministry of supplication
- Life-changing thoughts on prayer, Vol 1
- Life-changing thoughts on prayer, Vol 2
- Life-changing thoughts on prayer, Vol 3
- The centrality of prayer
-

- PRACTICAL HELPS FOR OVERCOMERS
- The use of time
- Retreats for spiritual progress
- Personal spiritual revival
- Daily dynamic encounters with God
- The school of truth
- How to succeed in the Christian life
- The Christian and money
- Deliverance from the sin of laziness
- The art of working hard
- Knowing God – The greatest need of the hour
- Restitution : An important message for the overcomers
- Revelation a must
- True repentance
- You can receive a pure heart today
- You can lead someone to the Lord Jesus today
- The overcomer as a servant of man
- You have a talent!
- The Making of Disciples
- The secret of spiritual fruitfulness
- The dignity of manual labour
-

- GOD, SEX AND YOU
- Enjoying the premarital life
- Enjoying the choice of your marriage partner
- Enjoying the married life
- Divorce and remarriage
- A successful marriage; the husband's making
- A successful marriage; the wife's making
-

- EVANGELISATION
- God's love and forgiveness
- Come back home my son; I still love you
- Jesus loves you and wants to heal you
- Come and see; Jesus has not changed!
- 36 reasons for winning the lost to Christ
- Soul winning, Volume 1
- Soulwinning, Volume 2
- Celebrity a mask
-

- **MAKING SPIRITUAL PROGRESS**
- Vision, burden, action
- The ministers and the ministry of the new covenant
- The cross in the life and ministry of the believer
- Knowing the God of unparalleled goodness
- Brokenness, the secret of spiritual overflow
- The secret of spiritual rest
- Making spiritual progress, Volume 1
- Making spiritual progress, Volume 2
- Making spiritual progress, Volume 3
- Making spiritual progress, Volume 4

- **PRACTICAL HELPS IN SANCTIFICATION**
- Deliverance from sin
- Sanctified and consecrated for spiritual ministry
- The Sower, the seed and the hearts of men
- Freedom from the sin of adultery and fornication
- The sin before you may lead to immediate death: Do not commit it!
- Be filled with the Holy Spirit
- The power of the Holy Spirit in the winning of the lost

- **OTHER BOOKS**
- Are you still a disciple of the Lord Jesus?
- A broken vessel
- The joy of begging to belong to the Lord Jesus : A testimony
- Laws of spiritual success, Volume 1
- Discipleship at any cost
- The shepherd and the flock
- Spiritual aggressiveness
- The secluded worshipper
- Deliverance from demons
- Inner healing
- No failure needs to be final
- You can receive the baptism into the Holy Spirit now
- Facing life's problems victoriously
- A word to the students
- The prophecy of the overthrow of the satanic prince of Cameroon
- The power to operate miracles

- **NEW BOOKS**
- Church Planting Strategies
- Delivrance from the Sin Of The Gluttony
- God Centredness
- God, Money And You
- In The Crucible For Service
- Issues Of The Heart
- Jesus Saves And Heals Today
- Leading A Local Church
- Meet The Liberator
- Power For Service
- Prayer And A Walk With God
- Prayer crusade Volume 1
- Revolutionary Thoughts On Spiritual Leadership
- Roots And Destinies
- Spiritual Fragrange
- Spiritual Gifts
- Spiritual Nobility
- The Art Of Worship
- The Believer's Conscience
- The Character And Personality Of The Leader
- The Leader & His God
- The Overthrow Of Principalities And Powers
- The Processes Of Faith
- The Spirit Filled Life
- Victorious Dispositions
- Walking With God
- Women Of The Glory Vol 1
- Women Of The Glory Vol 2
- Women Of The Glory Vol 3
- You, Your Team And Your Ministry

Imprimé en France par CPI
en septembre 2019

Dépôt légal : septembre 2019
N° d'impression : 154157